Cambridge Elements

Elements in Psychology and Culture
edited by
Kenneth D. Keith
University of San Diego

CULTURAL PSYCHOLOGY AND ACCULTURATION

Paweł Boski
SWPS University

CAMBRIDGE
UNIVERSITY PRESS

Shaftesbury Road, Cambridge CB2 8EA, United Kingdom

One Liberty Plaza, 20th Floor, New York, NY 10006, USA

477 Williamstown Road, Port Melbourne, VIC 3207, Australia

314–321, 3rd Floor, Plot 3, Splendor Forum, Jasola District Centre,
New Delhi – 110025, India

103 Penang Road, #05– 06/07, Visioncrest Commercial, Singapore 238467

Cambridge University Press is part of Cambridge University Press & Assessment,
a department of the University of Cambridge.

We share the University's mission to contribute to society through the pursuit of
education, learning and research at the highest international levels of excellence.

www.cambridge.org
Information on this title: www.cambridge.org/9781009451055

DOI: 10.1017/9781009451093

First published 2024

A catalogue record for this publication is available from the British Library.

ISBN 978-1-009-45105-5 Hardback
ISBN 978-1-009-45110-9 Paperback
ISSN 2515-3986 (online)
ISSN 2515-3943 (print)

Cultural Psychology and Acculturation

Elements in Psychology and Culture

DOI: 10.1017/9781009451093
First published online: February 2024

Paweł Boski
SWPS University

Author for correspondence: Paweł Boski, pboski@swps.edu.pl

Abstract: This Element offers a new theoretical model of acculturation within the general framework of cultural psychology. It is divided into four sections. First, cross-cultural and cultural orientations are contrasted. Each is illustrated with a detailed flowchart and step-by-step research procedures. Arguments are laid out for developing the psychology of acculturation within the cultural paradigm. The psychology of economic migration (EARN), separate from the psychology of acculturation (LEARN), is the theme of Section 2. Berry's model of acculturation preferences is discussed in Section 3. It serves as a contrasting reference point for the tripartite model of bicultural competencies, developed in Section 4. The three interconnected components are symbols, language, and values/practices. They characterize both enculturation and acculturation. As a second culture-learning process, acculturation is not restricted to immigration. It may take a vicarious (remote) shape in the home country. Reaching bicultural competencies and identities in the long run is the proposed outcome of acculturation.

Keywords: cultural psychology, acculturation, culture learning, bilingualism, bicultural identity

ISBNs: 9781009451055 (HB), 9781009451109 (PB), 9781009451093 (OC)
ISSNs: 2515-3986 (online), 2515-3943 (print)

Contents

Introduction

This Element intends to contribute to a new, alternative approach to acculturation psychology. Yet this important field at the intersection of culture and psychology is not autonomous; it must be integrated into a broader theoretical framework. Berry's approach to acculturation, which will serve as a major reference point for my work, is an excellent illustration of this starting point. The author is well known for his eco-cultural model (Berry, 1976, 1979), which appears in numerous handbook publications on cross-cultural psychology (CCP) (e.g., Berry et al., 2011, p. 11), and in his recent Elements volume (Berry, 2019, p. 7). In this model, two broad mechanisms of population adaptation are compared and contrasted: biological (e.g., genetic) and cultural transmission. Acculturation belongs to the latter class.

Before moving to the field of acculturation, I will outline a broader theoretical perspective, locating my approach within the context of cultural psychology. In doing this, I will draw on two earlier contributions (Boski, 2018, 2020) where cross-cultural and cultural paradigms of conducting psychological investigations were compared.

1 Cross-Cultural versus Cultural Psychology

The two models central to this Element and in the broader outlook (Poortinga, 2021) will be schematically outlined, compared, and contrasted. For precision, each will be illustrated with a study typical for its genre.

1.1 Cross-Cultural Psychology: Equivalence and Unpackaging in Comparative Studies

Cross-cultural psychology is a dominant field of research in culturally oriented psychology. It has its flagship journal (*Journal of Cross-Cultural Psychology* [*JCCP*]), association (International Association for Cross-Cultural Psychology [IACCP]), and fifty years of academic growth (Berry, Lonner & Best, 2022). Since early formulations in the *Handbook of Cross-Cultural Psychology* (Triandis, 1980) and Berry and colleagues (1997), the statistical methodology for handling the data collected in multiple parts (countries, regions) of the world has been the focus of researchers' attention. At the same time, the role of context for measured behavior was emphasized, particularly in the format of the eco-cultural model (Berry, 1976, 1979). Over decades, an evolution took place where the scope of pancultural projects and statistical methodological advancement inspired each other while the role of situational context shrank. Cross-cultural psychology became a discipline in which large teams of researchers distributed questionnaires, inventories, surveys, and (less often) tests in order to collect data in numerous countries while context became a vanishing point in their investigations. John Berry (2022) observed this tendency with critical remarks:

> [...] much of the more recent research published in cross-cultural [psychology] has spent very little time or effort on describing the ecological, cultural, learning, or situational contexts of psychological data [...] There has been a shift toward large-scale, pan-cultural studies in which the lead researcher does not carry the cultural work or have a first-hand experience in, or knowledge of the cultural context [...] If cross-cultural psychology is a search for culture–behavior links, then surely we need to spend equal time examining cultural contexts and behaviors. (p. 1005)

I fully agree with this diagnosis of the current state of CCP, expressed by one of its founders on the occasion of the fiftieth anniversary of the discipline. Berry (2019) lamented the drop of context, understood as field (anthropological) studies. However, not long ago, in his contribution to the Elements series, the author distanced himself from experimentation, where the stamp of context is equally present: "I have had some guides to assist in deciding what to do, including having fun and being useful when doing research. These guides have also assisted in deciding what not to do; **this is why I have never done an experiment** [bold mine – PB] or worked in a laboratory or clinic" (p. 4).

To conclude: the abandonment of context is a visible characteristic in current CCP, and because context is equivalent to culture, this creates a serious conceptual problem for the discipline. As further analysis in this section will show, context has been replaced by two other concerns: equivalence of measures and culture unpackaging. Relying almost exclusively on existing questionnaires, inventories, and scales, such studies represent what can best be called comparative psychometry. "Go back to field work" as a remedy suggested by Berry is not the only way to improve. Cultural experimentation is another option; particularly when this royal method in scientific psychology is to be applied in studies in nontraditional societies. In the meantime, the dominant paradigm of CCP research is illustrated in Figure 1. I will guide the reader through the steps of this model with illustrative support from a sixty-two-country research project by Bosson and colleagues (2021) on precarious manhood beliefs (PMB).

1.1.1 A Universal (Etic) Hypothesis

As a rule, cross-cultural studies begin with a universally formulated theory, or an *etic* assumption (Berry et al., 2011), concerning a phenomenon, process, or relationship. The authors of this investigation assumed that PMB is a universally recognized cultural phenomenon (stage [1a] of the flowchart in Figure 1). The paper starts with a quote: "Among most of the people that anthropologists are familiar with, true manhood is a precious and elusive status beyond mere maleness, a hortatory image that men and boys aspire to and that their culture demands of them as a measure of belonging." It goes on to say, "This theory further argues that the precariousness of their gender status leads men, relative to women, to experience higher levels of social anxiety and stronger motivation to compensate, sometimes via risky or aggressive posturing, when their gender status is challenged (Vandello & Bosson, 2013, p. 10)".

Let us assume that this claim has sufficient plausibility, although precarious womanhood beliefs are also convincingly documented. In many regions where traditional (preliterate) cultures have been sustained, female fertility is as much a virtue as it is precarious for biological reasons. In Nigeria, which ranks among the highest PMB countries, fertility is a condition of social and self-worth for women. It is young women, not men, who attend shrines and perform rituals to ascertain fertility and motherhood; failure in this domain is disastrous for their whole life.[1]

1.1.2 Original Measures

Let us move to the second step (1b) of the chain process depicted in Figure 1. Of the original scale prepared for North American studies, the authors selected four belief items (with the highest factor loadings) to be used in their pancultural investigation:

- Other people often question whether a man is a "real man."
- Some boys do not become men no matter how old they get.
- It is fairly easy for a man to lose his status as a man.
- Manhood is not assured – it can be lost.

These items are formulated broadly as if they could be used "all over the world." There is no clue to link the beliefs behind the statements to any culture of origin. At face value, the four-item scale is not a cultural variable because it does not refer to any context: scripts, socialization practices, routines, norms, or meta norms. It is not known wherein this precariousness lay: in physical prowess and sexuality, in the amount of alcohol a man can

---

[1] I am referring here to the cult of the Yoruba goddess Oshun (Esquerra, 2019; Wenger, 1990). Oshun is a fertility goddess, a source of hope for expecting mothers and young women yearning for motherhood. The literature on Oshun is large, and as the life of Susanne Wenger shows, the cult spills over ethnic borders. I had personal experience with the rituals in the sacred grove of Oshogbo during my years in Nigeria, 1977–84 (Boski, 2015).

consume, in economic success, or in social popularity. (Indeed, as we will learn later in this Element, between-country differences explain only 11 percent of its total variance.) It remains a priori unknown whether the formulations of these beliefs reflect how precariousness is defined in their cultures of origin (i.e., in North America).

There are other scales in the study I am referring to in which the emic nature of items is more prevalent and ideologically tagged.

> Hostile sexism and hostility toward men:
> Women seek to gain power by getting control over men.
> Women exaggerate the problems they have at work.
> When women lose to men in a fair competition, they typically complain about being discriminated against.
> Men will always fight to have greater control in society than women.
> Men act like babies when they are sick.
> Most men sexually harass women, even if only in subtle ways, once they are in a position of power over them.

> Benevolent sexism and benevolence toward men:
> Women should be cherished and protected by men.
> Men are incomplete without women.
> Women, compared to men, tend to have superior moral sensibility.
> Men are more willing to put themselves in danger to protect others.
> Every woman needs a male partner who will cherish her.
> A woman will never be truly fulfilled in life if she doesn't have a committed, long-term relationship with a man.

These items are expressions of current Western (emic) ideology where sexism is a concept charged with negative emotions, and when used for measuring purposes, it provides cultural evaluation rather than an objective description. This approach has been criticized by Boski (2022, ch. 10) as an implicit politicization of psychology. In particular, what is called *benevolent sexism* can, in cultural terms, be named *respectful courtesy*. Only one of the aforementioned items, framed as a popular belief – *Men are more willing to put themselves in danger to protect others* – offers a good example of widespread cultural practices. As it used to be with sea vessels sinking, and still is practiced during aircraft emergencies, women and children have precedence over men in rescue operations. Although this norm is part of a societal/organizational culture, I do not think it merits being called a culture of benevolent sexism. A positive alternative to an "omnipresent "sexism" is gender neutrality, equality, and distance.

All in all, universal hypotheses should be tested with universal measures. The examples show that some operationalizations are closer to meeting this postulate than others, yet it is generally very hard to formulate a verbal instrument that would be both culture-relevant and culture-free at the same time.

1.1.3 Back-Translation Procedures

Cross-cultural psychology subscribes to the idea of perfect measurement instruments typical in natural sciences, which can be used universally (always and everywhere). The problem, however, is that such measures are based on universal laws of nature, while all scales in CCP are statements expressed in natural languages, which differ across cultures and change over historical time.

Consider a traditional thermometer operating in the Celsius or Fahrenheit system. This instrument applies the universal law of thermal expansion, which regulates the height of mercury in response to ambient temperature. In contrast, a scale in psychology is a linguistic tool, and as such, it is a product of local culture, reflecting its limited terminological range and limited translatability. It is a contradiction if one attempts to build a universal science with the help of language-grounded cultural instruments. Still, some (e.g., Brislin, 1986) have believed that back translation is a panacea for linguistic multiplicity and that by applying this procedure researchers will obtain the desirable equivalence of meaning across contemporary cultures and across their historic times.

It is, however, naive to think that translation between any two languages (let alone numerous ones) could lead to identical meanings (Wierzbicka, 1999). As a linguist (psycho-semanticist), Wierzbicka did not preclude the possibility of a perfect translation, but she argued that this should be done through explications formulated in the natural semantic meta-language (NSM), and not directly from one language to another, as it is practiced in CCP. The NSM approach is an indirect, compromise approach to the problem of equivalence in translations. Regardless of whether the NSM lives up to expectations as an intermediary translation platform between two natural languages (Blumczyński, 2013), it provides researchers with a practical lesson for item construction. They should avoid complex, metaphoric, interpretative phrases and use simple terms resembling semantic primitives.

We must conclude that the goal of building a science of universal psychological laws resembling those of natural sciences, with the empirical phenomena expressed and measured in natural languages, is dubious. Linguistic measures render the phenomena under scrutiny culturally bound.

1.1.4 Research Consortia and Data Collection

Awareness of ethnocentric items and the linguistic problems of back translation seems to be growing. The late champion of cross-cultural psychometry Fons van de Vijver postulated during the last two IACCP conferences he attended (Van de Vijver, 2017, 2018 – unpublished presidential addresses), that scales for large cross-cultural projects should be prepared by consortia of researchers and professional linguists, proposing items relevant for their milieus. This approach would incur high costs compared to amateurish back translations, often done by postgraduate psychology students. I will share two potential items for the PMB, one coming from a Nigerian cultural context and another from a Polish one:

- It is shameful for a man not to be able to show his wealth equal to the level of his agemates (Nigeria).
- When a man turns out to be a boor with women, his image of a person deserving respect has been damaged (Poland; see the next section).

In the practice of large, pancultural projects, there is neither time nor patience on the side of the principal researcher to test and include such extra items in ready-made inventories. The role of collaborators who appear on impressive lists in publications is usually limited to linguistic back-translation procedures and to providing data collection, most likely among students at universities where these collaborators are employed. No other circumstantial evidence is sought or regarded as important.

1.1.5 From Psychometric Equivalence and Isomorphism to Testing Cross-Cultural Differences

In contrast to the marginal attention they pay to linguistic representativeness, translation, and semantic specificity of items, cross-cultural researchers devote much effort to establishing the statistical equivalence of their instruments. Testing procedures and their outcomes often becomes a major part of the results sections of reports. The issues of equivalence – its levels (configural, metric, and scalar), the statistical criteria for reaching them, and their consequences for further data analyses – have been sufficiently elaborated (e.g., He & Van de Vijver, 2012; Poortinga, 2021) and I feel exempt from discussing them in this Element. Suffice it to say that scalar equivalence, considered a condition for comparing group means, is difficult to obtain for many scales measuring abstract concepts such as values. A related and important issue in pancultural projects is the notion of isomorphism between individual and group levels of measurement. In the study on PMB, the question is whether the construct measuring individual beliefs about precarious manhood can be regarded as the same scale characterizing societal groups and the differences between them.

Only when the criteria of metric and scalar equivalence have been accomplished can researchers proceed to test hypotheses of relations between variables and group differences, respectively. These are strict conditions, resembling those imposed in natural sciences, where measures are based on laws of science, and not on a subjective sense of semantic consistency across languages. The basic assumption is that to compare precarious manhood (or any construct of this type) now and at any time cross-culturally, researchers should be equipped with measures of similar quality to meteorologists reporting ambient temperature across the world or to climatologists predicting dynamic weather phenomena in the future.

The authors of the PMB paper reported psychometrically successful outcomes of their analyses. Indeed, the title scale and four measures of sexism were found cross-culturally equivalent and isomorphic between individual and national groups (configural and partially metric levels), confirming the first set of their hypotheses, which corresponds to stage [6] in the model presented in Figure 1. This allows passing to the last stage, stage [7], of the model.

1.1.6 Unpackaging Cultural Differences

The *why* question may be of more relevance in science than mere fact-finding. If researchers are successful in demonstrating differences between the studied samples or different profiles of relations between variables in these samples, then the need to explain the causality of these effects unavoidably arises. In CCP researchers' jargon, it is called *unpackaging* (Bond & Tadeschi, 2001). Often, unpackaging is done with hierarchical modeling, where relations found at the individual level are explained by culture-level differences (e.g., subjective well-being [SWB] is predicted by personal scores on horizontal individualism, which is moderated by culture-level individualism; Diener et al., 1995). In the case of the PMB paper, the unpackaging was executed after establishing isomorphism between individual and cultural levels of the scale.

Next, two macro-level indices – the Human Development Index (HDI) and the Global Gender Gap Index (GGGI) – were used to explain the differences in the PMB country-level differences. The GGGI is a combined measure of gender parity in economic participation and opportunity, educational attainment, health and survival, and political empowerment. The researchers found that countries scoring high in global gender parity (high GGGI) – for example, Scandinavian countries – were significantly lower in PMB and all sexist scales; also, clusters

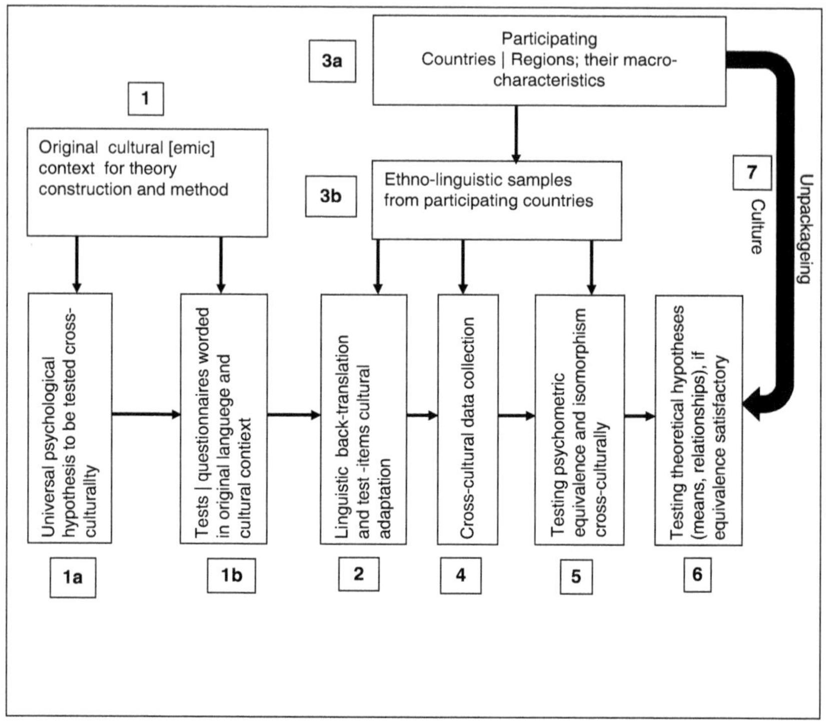

Figure 1 The flowchart research model of cross-cultural psychology

Note: All notations of the flowchart stages from stage [1a] to stage [6] appear in the main text, where they are given full explanations.

of PMB showed regional proximity corresponding with their positions on both the HDI and the GGGI.

As with any publication, the paper on precarious manhood and sexism has its limitations. I will briefly discuss them from the perspective of a general CCP model and their possible applications to the psychology of acculturation. First, with an isomorphic alignment, one cannot leap from an individual point of view to the cultural level of a phenomenon manifesting itself as a shared value or belief syndrome, or a script. When a country (e.g., Nigeria) scores high on PMB, it may make rituals of passage more likely for many adolescents, but the country score itself does not represent this particular (or any other) cultural arrangement in this domain. Similarly, a low percentage of between-group variance does not necessarily indicate that a phenomenon under scrutiny shows predominantly intraindividual differences, but rather that cultures are heterogeneous, falling under opponent scripts.

Thus a large, sixty-two-country project may give some guidance in terms of cultural distance affecting individuals entering the acculturation process from a high-PMB region to a low-PMB region – for example, from Nigeria or Kosovo to Finland (or the other way around). But because acculturation is always about (re-, un-)learning specific scripts, this broad overview needs to be translated into contextual variables, missing as much as needed (Berry, 2022).[2]

This section started with a reference to Berry's eco-cultural level, where acculturation was introduced, often as a factor in overcoming ecological determinants of human behavior in populations. This would typically apply to colonial experience in traditional societies, where Western schooling, language, or laws had been imported to Indigenous populations who did not change their residence. But this encouraging initial approach was not continued in the field of acculturation, which started in earnest in the 1980s (except perhaps for earlier studies on Indigenous populations). Acculturation psychology, as it is largely practiced today, took shape some forty years ago, following the CCP model described in this section. Berry introduced this approach in his IACCP presidential address (Berry, 1985) and scholars have continued applying it in collaborative research projects ever since (e.g., Berry et al., 2006; Berry et al., 2018). Subsequently, acculturation has become the study of attitudes (beliefs, preferences) conducted on immigrants originating from various home countries and settling in host countries. These attitudes are believed to be universally valid and researchers claim that measuring them in any home–host country combination will result in establishing the general laws of the discipline.

1.2 Cultural Psychology and Cultural Experiment

The starting point of cultural psychology is largely different from that of the cross-cultural paradigm. Here it is culture – not a psychological theory – that becomes the springboard for research problems and hypotheses. Any aspect of culture may offer this impulse. The inspiration may come even from such an abstract discipline as philosophy, which led to one of the most creative endeavors in recent decades: the work on analytical and holistic cognitive styles. It started with an observation that two great civilizations – the Confucian civilization in East Asia and the Greco-Roman civilization in Europe – differed remarkably in their philosophical roots since antiquity (Chmielewski, 2009; Nisbett, 2003). While Greek philosophers developed a system of classical logic and reasoning, Confucius and Taoists concentrated instead on paradoxes and contradictions and the web of interconnections between objects (see also Boski, 2022/2009, ch. 9; Peng, Spencer-Rodgers & Nian, 2006).

---

2 Since I mentioned Finland as the country ranking lowest in PMB and second lowest in the GGGI, it appears as a prototype for safe gender egalitarianism. Perhaps for many men it would be a rather shocking scenario where in some clubs women initiate dancing with single men.

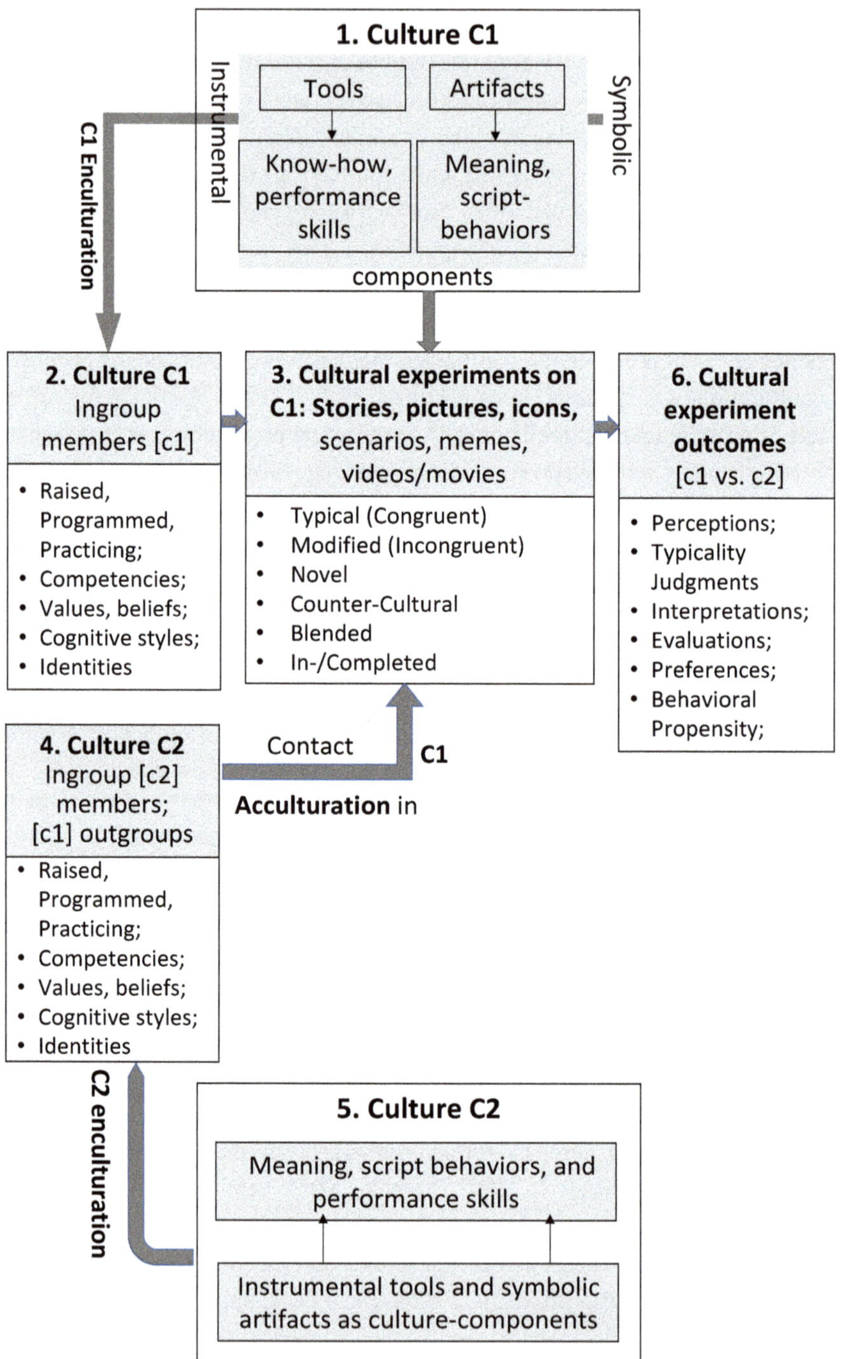

Figure 2 A flowchart research model of cultural psychology

A large number of studies on causal thinking and attributions, classification, memory, perception, and aesthetics derived from these philosophical premises. Participants in psychological studies are not philosophers, and they may have not taken any courses in philosophy, yet they have been trained incidentally in what their cultures regard as proper ways of reasoning and perceiving reality in everyday practice. In general, any cultural domain may serve as the starting point for cultural psychological investigation. Figure 2 outlines the research paradigm of cultural psychology.

1.2.1 Culture C1, Its Repository, and Its In-Group Actors/Observers [1, 2]

Culture is understood in this Element as (i) an overlay and continuous transformation of humanity's natural environment, (ii) a noosphere of symbolic meaning (knowledge) evolving in a cumulative and creative development process, and (iii) a normative transgression from actual to ideal life. Culture is transmitted in societal channels whereby members learn and acquire their cognitive competencies and behavioral skills, beliefs, and valuation systems. Accordingly, the cultural repository at the top of Figure 2 is divided into instrumental (left) and symbolic parts (on the right), the latter being central to cultural identity. Normative-behavioral culture is composed of many sectors and organized in what Chirkov (2020) calls sociocultural models (SCMs) – that is, scripts of goal-oriented, institutionalized interactions (Schank & Abelson, 1995; Wierzbicka, 1994, 1999). It is important that SCMs and scripts are shared intersubjectively and can be formalized as elements of objective cultural reality.

Sociocultural models and scripts become a matter of enculturation (Box 2 on the left of Figure 2) so members of a society learn what is normatively expected, how to interpret situations falling into such scripts, and how to communicate with others, express approval, and implement corrective, meta-normative measures. For enculturated members, SCMs and scripts become their psychological reality; such persons are equipped with cognitive, emotional, and motivational processes regulating a set of interactions with coactors. Because scripts are (inter)action structures, they are very suitable for use in experimental studies, in live or recorded conditions.

1.2.2 Cultural Experiments on C1 [3]

The cultural experiment is an important methodological concept that I have introduced for the type of cultural psychology presented in this Element (Boski, 2018, 2020). As with any other experiment, it must entail at least two conditions. In the simplest design, one of these conditions consists of an exact script replica, while the other is its intentional modification, ranging from a slight to a large countercultural reversal (or violation). The first condition provides material for confirmatory evidence about the script operating at the level of culture C1 among local participants. In logical terms, it creates a sufficient condition for confirmation. The modified condition is more complex and less obvious. Script reversal creates a more stringent, necessary condition (*sine qua*) for its validation (for logical foundations of this argument, see Boski, 2018 and Johnson-Laird & Wason, 1985). This **logic of disconfirmation** assumes that a stronger proof of cultural reality occurs when participants confronted with the denial of important script elements still hold to what their normative standards oblige them to do. In simple terms, a cultural experiment consists of "experimenting with culture"; it should demonstrate that participants will not be sidetracked by a researcher's effort to induce denial of script elements.

I will illustrate the idea of cultural experiments with a class demonstration I have repeated more than 100 times during introductory lectures (Boski, 2018). This involves applying a simple script in a [request → compliance] format: if people are approached with a culturally appropriate request (p), they will do what is requested (q). Based on my native knowledge of and the literature on Polish culture (Boski, 2022, ch. 11), I assumed that the script to be tested operates in the following format: *Moving heavy objects* (p) *is a male task* (q) *so men should be requested and expected to carry out such tasks*. Being so obvious, this script was not verified in its logically sufficient condition: "May I ask two men *[q]* to move a cabinet or a blackboard stand from the hallway to the class?"[3] Instead, I attempted script disconfirmation by slightly changing the request format: "May I ask two women [~q], to move the object (a cabinet or a blackboard stand) from the hallway to the class?"

Logically and culturally, this change of gender address would presume that the object to be moved was light [~p]. However, if no reaction came from the female part of the class, we would have to conclude that the request was based on the false assumption of the object's light weight (~p) and was not complied with as culturally inappropriate. Class demonstrations under that modified request condition were performed with Polish students on ninety-six occasions; in eighty-six occurrences not a single woman responded. In all of those trials, male dyads spontaneously complied with the request (Boski, 2020). This repeated result offers a clear demonstration that people do not respond literally to script violations, but they attempt to apply some corrective measures. The

---

[3] In logical terms, p stands for "culturally appropriate request"; q stands for compliance with this request; $\sim$ = the negation sign for p or for q. The formula $[(p \rightarrow q) \times p] \rightarrow q$ identifies *modus ponens*, a **sufficient** condition for validating the script; $[(p \rightarrow q) \times \sim q] \rightarrow \sim p$ identifies *modus tolens*, a **necessary** condition in script validation.

power of script validation obtained through its unsuccessful negation seems much stronger than by confirmation in a sufficient condition.

1.2.3 Culture B Out-Group Actors/Observers [4–5]

While designing a cultural experiment for C1, in-group members may require the original script reversal; the same effect may be obtained by exposing C2 members, unfamiliar with that culture, to its intact format. For them, it may be a brief intercultural contact or a step in the acculturation process. Similarly, what appears to be a counter-script to locals may not elicit a backlash among out-culture members. Here again, the class demonstration *May I ask two women …* comes as a relevant source of evidence: on seventeen out of eighteen attempts performed in Western European countries, two female students moved the indicated object to the class (Boski, 2020). Even if the request posed to them was awkward (see next caption), they did not experience script violation because *Males are responsible to move heavy objects* was foreign to their cultural reality.

Entering interaction with culture **C1** members, or visiting their country, members of out-culture **C2** will unavoidably come into contact with a new reality unfamiliar to them, making them prone to misunderstandings. Similarly, their cultural programming may elicit behaviors very unusual in the new environment. The literature on intercultural training abounds in such scenarios, which are called *critical incidents* (Cushner & Brislin, 1996; Thomas, 2002).

Were it not for researchers' *cultural blindness* (Berry, 1999), which may impair this task, designing a cultural experiment by selecting a script and constructing its reversal appears not to be a challenging endeavor. Exploiting events brought in from a distant cultural reality is the opposite way of reaching the same goal by local script modification. Let me share two experiences from my professional life with international students in Poland that exemplify these ideas. Never before in my fifty years of teaching at Polish or Western universities have similar episodes happened to me:

1. (i) In an online consultation during COVID-19, and during my quarantine isolation, a student from South Asia offered to do grocery shopping for me. (ii) Another person from South Asia brought lunch for me to the office during a face-to-face consultation.
2. (i) When shopping in an African grocery store in Warsaw, I met a Nigerian former student; after a brief conversation, I walked down the aisle to pick up some goods, leaving the food basket behind. When I came back to the counter, that person had paid for all of those products.
(ii) When another Nigerian person and I were leaving my office together, they picked up my computer bag and carried it to my car in the parking lot.

These incidents exemplify the *diffusion* pole on a dimension with *specificity* at the other extreme (Trompenaars & Hampden-Turner, 1997). Power distance and respect/politeness for a senior person of higher status are of importance too. What is significant here is that such incidents offer ready-made scenarios for cultural experiments with Euro-American participants.

1.2.4 Outcome Variables and Results [6]

The last part of Figure 2 contains a list of measures used as dependent variables in cultural experiments. They include culture perception or interpretation and semantic understanding of acted or observed episodes, typicality assessments and evaluations, emotions elicited by unfolding events, memory, inferential judgments and predictions, preferences and identifications, and action tendencies and tolerance to script departures. The dependent measures in a cultural experiment are usually related to the pictorial, behavioral material being presented in such a study.

Essential in any cultural experiment is the contextual status of dependent variables; they are localized amid what is seen and done, here and now. These are not abstract scales unrelated to what the participants may be thinking and doing right now, or in general. Consequently, the problem of equivalence, so vital in cross-cultural research, is of much less importance when participants are asked the meaning of, their feelings about, and their inferential judgments of what they see and hear.

1.2.5 A Request → Compliance Cultural Experiment Based on May I Ask Two Women

I will now demonstrate the design and results of a cultural experiment that followed the *May I ask two women* scenario described earlier in this section (Boski, 2020). Four video recordings followed a 2 [gender-addressed **request**: females vs. males] x 2 [gender **compliance**: females vs. males] research design. The scenarios for four 2.5-minute videos were prepared beforehand with roles played by a pair of instructors and a class of twenty students, all of them Poles.

Teachers and students are seen entering a seminar room. A female instructor (Dr. X) greets them and introduces her male colleague (Dr. Y), with whom she will conduct a workshop on "The Importance of Culture and Nature in Shaping the Human Psyche." This topic appears on the screen behind her. Then she defers to her male companion, who announces that the class will be split into two teams, each working on arguments favoring one side of the culture–nature debate. After explaining some technical details, the man makes an offhand remark that a flipchart stand would be useful to write the arguments on, and he turns to the class with a request: "May I ask two women(men) to please move in a board from the room next door?" Next, after a short interval of *decision-making*, prearranged dyads of male or female students respond by complying with the request. The compliance may be consistent or inconsistent with the gender-typed request. After moving the stand into the class, the students are thanked by the male instructor.

Polish and English students participated in the study, watching one video and commenting on its cultural content. English subtitles of conversations led in Polish were provided. Dependent variables followed the list in the last box of Figure 2: typicality judgments, interpretations, script and actor evaluations, personal preferences, and self-motivations. Two results are presented in Figure 3. Polish and English participants are compared in three request conditions.[4]

As Figure 3a illustrates, a highly significant interaction was obtained between participants' characteristics (culture and gender) and gender-targeted requests on request appropriateness.[5] For English female participants, any request whereby gender would be mentioned was equally unacceptable; only *May I ask two persons/people* (which did not appear in any video) was normatively correct. This was not so for Poles, for whom the male-targeted request was about equally acceptable as that for the neutral-gender request, regardless of their gender. The largest simple effect for the two ethnic samples was that concerning the male-targeted request. The large gap between Poles of either gender and English female participants confirms the hypothesis that *physical tasks = masculine jobs* for Poles, but not for English participants.

The profiles of request normative appropriateness are reflected in the sense of duty participants declared they would feel if a similar situation occurred to them (Figure 3b). Polish males felt a stronger motivation to comply than Polish and English women. Their sense of duty was particularly strong when the request was male-addressed, leaving women to stay idle. Although women were more likely to respond to request addressed to their gender, it generated considerable motivation among men too.

Other cultural experiments in our lab. In collaboration with my colleagues and students, I have conducted many cultural experiments over many years. Gender issues were present in most of them (Boski, Van de Vijver & Miluska, 1999; Boski, Struś & Tlaga, 2004; Boski & Antosiewicz, 2006); others included religious icons (goddesses) or religious caricatures (Boski, 2018, experiment 5). Studies on Nigerian ethnic prototypes (Boski, 1988a) and African bicultural characters in the process of acculturation (Boski & Baran, 2018) completed the

---

[4] Because the number of English male participants was very small, analyses were conducted for English women and Poles of both gender categories. Also, a gender-neutral request condition was included. That condition did not appear on video recordings but was added as a response category.

[5] All reported results from this study are significant at $p < 0.001$, and effect sizes (η^2) are very high.

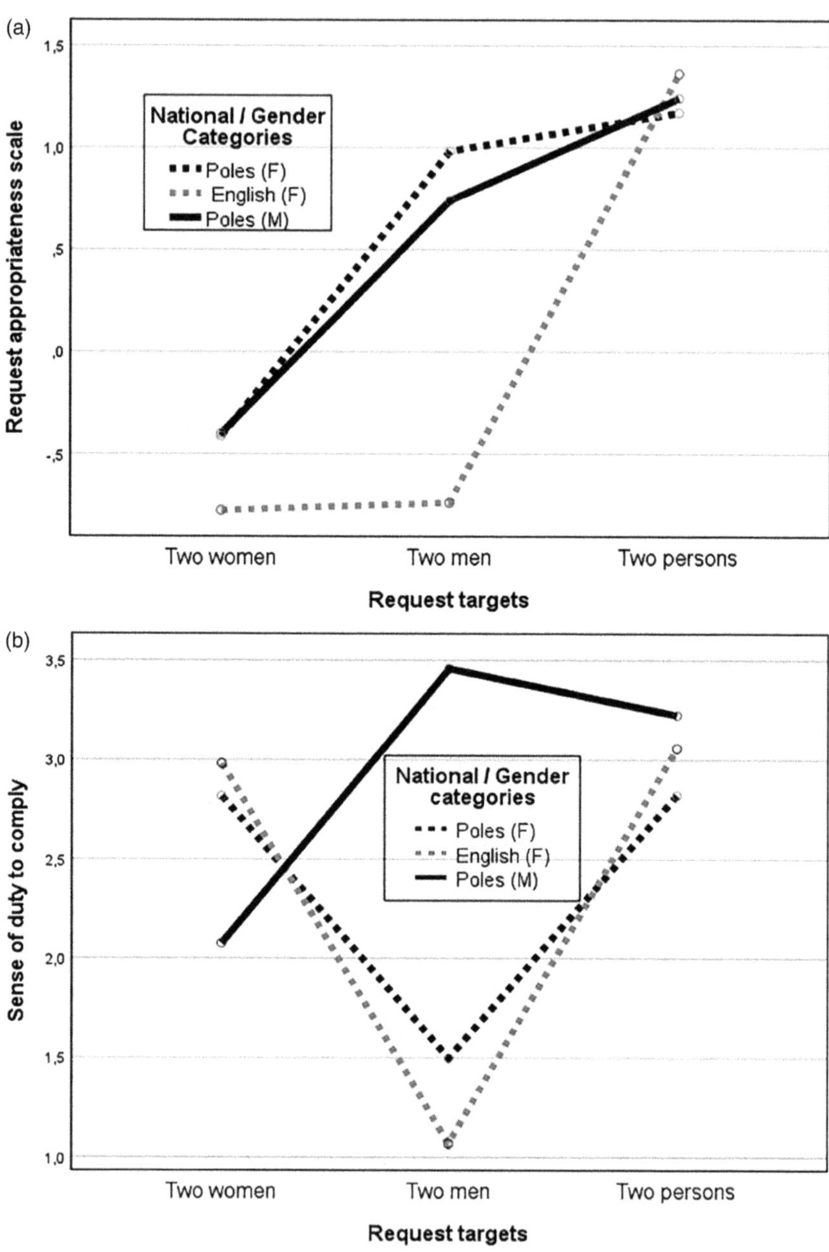

Figure 3a. Appropriateness of lecturer's requests addressed to three target categories. Polish–English cross-cultural and cross-gender comparisons. **b.** Sense of self-duty (motivation to comply) under three types of requests. Polish–English cross-cultural, and cross-gender comparisons

list. In most studies on gender issues, Polish traditional scripts articulated elevated women's roles, locally accepted, and regarded reluctantly by participants from Western nations.

The common elements in those investigations were video materials representing cultural scripts and their modification. It is a purposeful methodology because culture can be best accessed in pictorial recordings of ongoing interactions between its members. This applies to a broad range of situations: from mundane actions (e.g., meals with a group of people) to sacred, symbolic, and ceremonial events. Cultural experiments run on motion pictures open vast opportunities to study culture perception, typicality and inferential judgments, script (mis)understandings, personal preferences and evaluations, and cultural identity. They offer a smooth transition to acculturation research. What is important is that these experiments can get by without the context-free scales used in CCP. The questions participants answer are most like objective tests (about knowledge and understanding) or specific, context-related preferences and feelings.

1.3 Cross-Cultural and Cultural Psychology: A Possible Cross-Fertilization?

In past decades, the history of relations between CCP and CP (cultural psychology) was tense and sometimes even antagonistic. This was clearly expressed in works by Cole (1996) and Schweder (1995). Similar sentiments were reciprocated from the IACCP side. The two models presented and discussed in the last two sections also attest to the differences. But, animosity and a sense of self-righteousness are not very constructive in science. While respecting differences and adhering to their research preferences, psychologists of both orientations can find a common ground for collaboration. Poortinga, who for years represented a radical wing in CCP, has recently adopted a moderate position in this debate: " In the past twenty years, many researchers in the schools of cultural psychology and cross-cultural psychology have become less adversarial about one another's research and theoretical perspectives and have started to emphasize common interests and complementarity of approaches" (Poortinga, 2021, p. 16).

1.3.1 From a Pancultural Research Project to an In-Depth Cultural Experiment

To recall, the study exemplifying the CCP model, conducted in sixty-two countries, was dedicated to PMB and related gender constructs. Those were clustered into four regions spread along PMB and the GGGI. The cluster of high PMB and a high ranking on the GGGI is where Muslim countries dominate (e.g., Iran, Pakistan, and parts of Nigeria). The opposite cluster of low PMB and a low ranking on the GGGI includes Nordic and Western European countries. Based on these results, cultural psychologists may select Nigeria and Finland for a cultural experiment designed according to scripted gender roles (e.g., in a video format). A Nigerian script could contrast a woman carrying goods for a market sale on her head and a baby attached on her back, with a man (presumably her husband) following her while carrying a sun-protecting umbrella over his head. A Finnish script could present a man nursing a baby while his female partner relaxes on a sofa, watching TV. The experiment could be run along the lines presented in *May I ask two women …*

1.3.2 From a Cultural Experiment to a Pancultural Cross-Cultural Psychology Study

In this reversed format of collaboration, materials from the Polish–English experiment can be used by expanding its sample to a large cross-cultural project. Using original scripts makes it possible to explore inferred motivations and intentions behind observed behaviors (e.g., Would a male actor fail or assert his manhood by responding to a request addressed to women? Is relieving a woman of a tedious chore an act of benevolent sexism, or courteous respect?).

Our discussion so far has served as an introduction setting the stage for the psychology of migration and acculturation. We have now reached a point suitable for opening the main section of this Element, locating it in the context of cultural psychology, prolonged contact with natives, and acquisition of a new culture.

2 Psychology of Economic Migrations

Before I proceed with the presentation of my theoretical approach to acculturation, two preparatory steps are necessary. The first is its distinction from economic migration; the next is a brief discussion on the dominant model in the field.

2.1 EARN versus LEARN

The vast majority of studies on acculturation cover all populations of migrants and sedentary minority communities entering contact with majoritarian societies. These populations are economic immigrants, sojourners, refugees, and aboriginal or ethnolinguistic groups. Yet migrants of various categories prevail in most studies.

Migration studies form a popular topic when one peruses the extant literature in other disciplines of the social sciences, but not in psychology.[6] Acculturation, on the other hand, looks to be reserved for psychology. Yet the phenomena and

---

[6] Journals such as the *Journal of Migration and Integration*, *Journal of Ethnic and Migration Studies*, *Migration Studies*, and a host of others manage without even mentioning our keyword "acculturation."

processes under investigation on both sides of the academic demarcation line are not separate. The overlapping interests are work and economic adaptation, and intergroup relations and attitudes. We should address the question of whether the distinction between migration studies and acculturation is mainly terminological or covers a more substantial difference. In formulating a positive answer to the second part of this question, I propose an important conceptual disentanglement between economic migration and acculturation.

Two catchword verbs, EARN versus LEARN, reflect this differentiation. Their cross-section in Table 1 depicts four conditions of contact with the second country's job market and/or culture. The third criterion of this taxonomy is sedentary (the home country) versus migratory (the host country) residence.

The three dichotomized criteria exhibit the complex reality in a simplified way, enabling us to classify individuals into clearly distinct categories, ranging from zero contact with the out-group world (in a sedentary monocultural environment or migratory seclusion) to full immersion in its economic or symbolic (cultural) aspects. Attention should be particularly drawn to incongruent categories: first, where intercultural contact coincides with sedentary residence, and second, where migration does not lead to intercultural contact.

The former category has become particularly salient in recent decades. It comprises children from preschool to high school age and young adults who attend international schools, and, later, universities. Here we also have employees of multinational corporations that open regional branches with foreign languages and organizational cultures locally implemented. On the other hand, large numbers of economic migrants and expatriates may live in separate/sheltered conditions, where their contact with the local culture is intentionally or practically minimized. (This also applies to their family members who remain out of the workforce.)

Based on these conceptual distinctions, the psychology of economic migration (EARN) can and should be researched separately from acculturation psychology (LEARN). Each of them is focused on a different aspect of foreignness: material versus symbolic conditions of societal life. Table 2 presents a systematic comparison of the two modes of relationships with the foreign world.

The main (if not the only) goal of millions of economic migrants who have populated selected regions of the world (now called the Global North) during the past 150 years is improvement in their individual and family economic situation, which is usually marked by extreme poverty in the homeland. Their energy is concentrated on working for a wage and saving their earnings. All other activities are superfluous, and if costly, then irrational. All activities that serve cultural learning are costly and as such are disregarded by economic migrants. Acculturation can be seen as an investment in one's future; in the short

Table 1 EARN and LEARN in first and second cultures, and sedentary versus migratory life conditions

EARN	Sedentary in native C1 culture		Migrants to C2 culture	
	LEARN (second culture)		**LEARN (second culture)**	
	No	Yes	No	Yes
No: Students, retirees	C1: Single culture enculturation	**En-** and **Ac-culturation**: Bicultural education (L2 |C2 school learning)	Immigrant preschool children; elderly family members residing with their adult immigrant children	**Acculturation**: Migrants' children attending national and ethnic schools; international students-sojourners
Yes: Employees	Working in a monocultural environment: institution and living in a mono-cultural community	**Acculturation:** Working in multinational corporations (with second language and second culture organization) Communication with international colleagues	(i) Economic migrants of low-skill jobs, (ii) expatriates, experts; both with **minimal** intercultural contacts living in ethnic camps or communities	**Acculturation:** Immigrant professionals performing highly specialized jobs in L2 and adapting to the demands of local organizational culture

Table 2 EARN and LEARN: Comparing the two modes of contact with the second country's reality

Domains	EARN: Economic migrants	LEARN: Sojourners/learners
Priority goal	Improvement of material standards of living	Learning and acquiring competences in second culture
Country selection	Based on economic considerations: Prospects for satisfactory work and pay, ease of legalization	Interest in and preferences for language and other aspects of second culture, including instrumental reasons
Earning versus spending money	Earning as the central motive for leaving home country and settling down in host country, cutting expenses	Earning minimal if any, spending sizeable quotas for education and culture exploration
Second language and culture	Limited to basic job requirements, incidental acquisition, indifference	Central, usually mastered in formal instruction, intrinsic interest in second culture
Social contacts	Mostly with home country in-groups, isolation from local majority	Often with the second culture members, native speakers, immersion programs
Lifestyle	Work hard to maximize earnings and trim expenses	Demanding but enjoyable cognitive activities and progress in skill acquisition
Stress	To maintain job and income, fatigue, and exhaustion	Acculturative: To understand and perform well, to manage conflicting normative demands
Duration	Short: Seasonal/returning workers. Long: Permanent/naturalized immigrants	Short: Course students, scholarship exchange visitors. Long: Full-time students, residents, or visitors
Field of study	Social sciences of migration: Economy, sociology, psychology, demography, history	Cultural psychology of acculturation, foreign language education, and bilingualism

run, it incurs immediate costs while the payoffs are delayed. Words uttered by one of the immigrants embellished my paper ten years ago: "We come to live here to earn your money and not to learn your language" (Boski, 2013). With all of these conceptual distinctions made, a pressing question surfaces: when and how are immigrants transformed into acculturated individuals in their host countries? The answer is complex. Acculturation is a lifelong process and its profile is fuzzy. To some extent, it is even a matter of generation. Suffice it to say now that economic motives that dominate at the onset may stay this way for decades, with room for minimal acculturation only.

2.2 Psychology of Economic Migration: A Theoretical Model and Empirical Evidence

I have developed a model for the psychology of economic migration (Boski, 2010, 2013. 2022, ch. 13), which is summarized in ten theorems with empirical evidence supporting them.[7]

2.2.1 The Economic and Sociodemographic Context

T_1. Improving standards of economic well-being. The primary goal of temporary or permanent migration is to substantially improve individual and family economic standing when that is impossible to accomplish in the region and country of origin. Economically advanced countries' labor markets offer such opportunities.

T_2. Legal status. Labor demand in job markets is met either by legal migration within the framework of international agreements and contract regulations or by illegal (undocumented) migration.

These two initial theorems do not require psychological research. T_1 is axiomatic. Economic migration is driven by push and pull factors that are of an economic and sociodemographic nature: unemployment, overpopulation, and poverty in countries of origin correspond with labor demand, population decline, aging societies, and affluence in receiving countries (Bodvarsson & van de Berg, 2013).

T_3. Sectors of low-skilled labor. Job markets open to immigrants during economic prosperity and growth and also due to demographic factors when population growth in the host country is insufficient to meet labor demand. Job sectors open to immigrants are low in skill and pay, not attractive for the citizens of the host majority. There is overwhelming evidence that migrants are overrepresented in low-skilled jobs. Chmielewska (2015) found that 75 percent of Polish immigrants in the United Kingdom, Ireland, Germany, and the

---

[7] This model is formulated to cover the category of economic migrants in its *pure sense* – that is, labor flows from less to more developed countries. It does not apply to expatriates who represent a reverse flow of specialists sent on attractive contracts to developing countries and living there as foreign elites.

Netherlands were employed in such vocations. The same author and her colleagues found 70 percent of Ukrainian immigrants in Poland perform simple, unskilled jobs, and another 23 percent work as skilled laborers (Chmielewska, Dobroczek & Puzynkiewicz, 2016). Low-skilled jobs do not require acculturation but, demand universal physical competencies.

T_4. Professional degradation. Because immigrants come from technologically retarded regions of the world, their professional competencies documented by certificates, degrees, and diplomas are not duly recognized in hosting countries. The trade-off they accept for relatively profitable jobs is professional and status degradation. The high-density distribution of migrants in low-skilled jobs is not only the effect of their lower education levels but also the evaluation of their degrees/diplomas as nonequivalent with those awarded in the country of settlement (a medical doctor from Poland or Nigeria may not be recognized as a doctor in the United States or Canada).

Limitations. Exceptions to T_3 and T_4 occur. With shortages of educated specialists, criteria for immigrants' acceptance become relaxed (e.g., physicians originating from less advanced countries may not be required to repeat all of their exams and internship before being allowed to practice medicine in member states of the European Union [EU] or Canada).

T_5. Wage differences and incentives. Jobs on low-skill/low-wage scales are attractive enough if these offers surpass immigrants' comparison levels anchored in the job markets of their home countries. Indeed, earlier studies by Chmielewska and her colleagues (Chmielewska, 2015; Chmielewska et al., 2016) and more recent Eurostat and Polishstat (GUS) data for 2021 show that the ratio of minimal (per hour and monthly) and average wages in Poland to those in Ukraine and in Germany to those in Poland are in the range of 3:1 (accordingly, the ratio of those indices in Germany to those in Ukraine becomes 9:1). These are very strong incentives, activating individual resources for hard work. While the first five theorems belong to the socioeconomic *hardware* of migration realities, the second five specify *psychological* conditions.

2.2.2 Economic Immigrants' Hard Work

T_6. American Dream. An American Dream ideology was created as a cultural belief system providing optimism that by individual effort and diligence, the economic status of immigrants will go from a penniless position to that of a millionaire (Adams, 2012/1931).

T_7. Work effort. Filling the gap between self-imposed and/or family (social) expectations and a low starting point necessitates (i) concentration on high effort in job performance (e.g., low wages are compensated by overtime),

(ii) trimming daily expenses (thrift), and (iii) saving all possible means to satisfy the future goals that led to migration.

We have collected ample evidence on hard work characterizing immigrants (Boski, 2013, 2022, ch. 13). In several studies, we used the International Personality Item Pool (IPIP) to measure self-and/or observer-perceived changes due to immigration. Conscientiousness was the key dimension, interpreted as work diligence and effort.

In Study #1 (Boski, 2013), Polish and Irish participants living in their home countries served as observers of a selected colleague at work whom they knew for at least a year. Polish immigrants to Ireland constituted the third group. All participants completed IPIP scales for the target person. Polish immigrants were rated much higher in conscientiousness than the targets residing in their home countries. I consider this result very important because it denies the impact of either enculturation or acculturation. Immigrants' magnified conscientiousness is neither a product of their home culture nor of the host country's culture; it is an effect of their chosen migratory life goals.

In Study #2, we shifted the design from observers' reports to self-reporting. The direction and degree of change were measured at two points in the interval stretching between just before leaving Poland and at the time of investigation in the British Isles. Each item had two formats: (i) a present or past self-assessment (e.g., *I am/I was always well prepared.*); and (ii) a relative change measured prospectively (e.g., *Now, I am more/less prepared than I used to be in Poland*) or retrospectively (e.g., *I used to be more/less prepared than I am here where I live now*). Thus, in the **prospective** condition, the present level of each item was a sum of its past level and self-perceived change; in the **retrospective** condition, the past level was a sum of its present level and self-perceived change (counted backward).

Results for conscientiousness confirmed the findings from Study #1. There was a highly significant increment in this dimension, representing more hard work in the present than in the premigration past. That main effect was also contingent on temporal orientation: the upward change in conscientiousness was more pronounced prospectively than in a retrospective condition. These results can be seen in Figure 4a. (A noticeable tendency for overall positive personality changes in agreeableness, cognitive openness, extraversion, and emotional stability was also found.)

Conscientiousness, interpreted as hard work or effort, is the key variable characterizing economic migrants working abroad. Compared to local colleagues at work, Poles in Germany assessed themselves as deficient on four IPIP dimensions, except conscientiousness. Piętka (2015) obtained interesting results in two categories of adult siblings. In her control group, both lived in

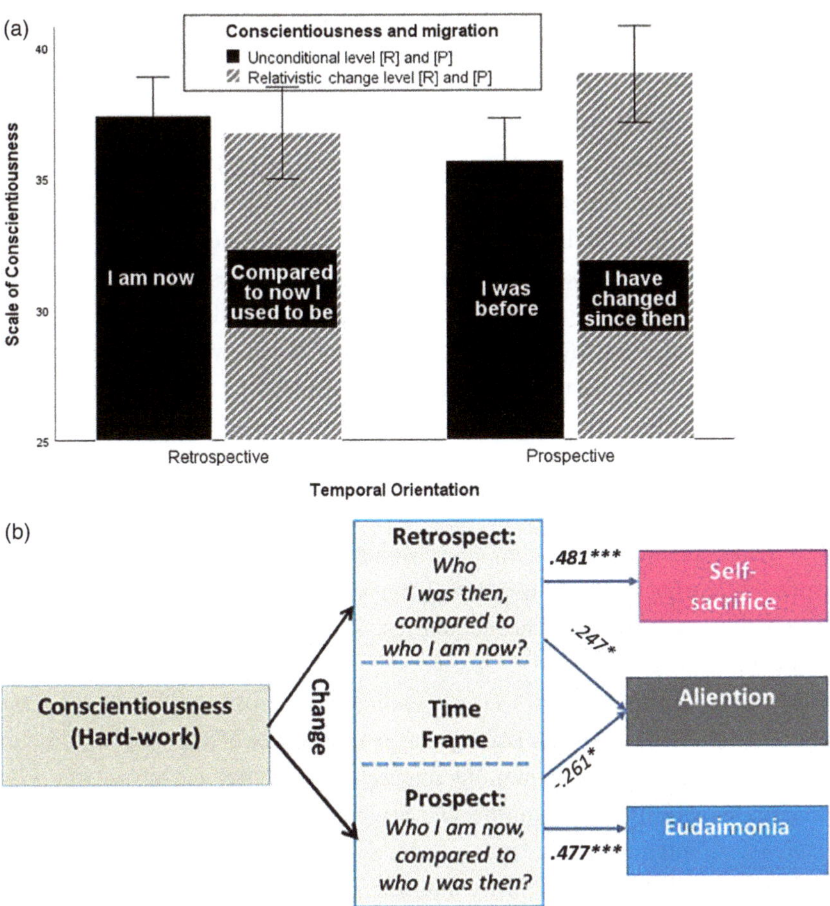

Figure 4 a. Retrospective and prospective self-perceived changes in conscientiousness (hard work) and **b.** their consequences among economic immigrants (Poles in the British Isles)

Poland but away from their parental homes. Randomly, one of them provided a self-report while the other used IPIP as that person's observer. The other category of siblings consisted of dyads in which one person was an immigrant who played the role of the self-reporting actor; his/her brother or sister, residing in Poland, served as the former's observer.

For all five personality dimensions, there was congruence between self- and observer reports among inside-the-country dyads (range $0.46 \leq r \leq 0.59$). Those coefficients were much lower when one sibling was an immigrant ($-0.15 \leq r \leq 0.14$), the lowest negative being found for conscientiousness. Why did the inter-sibling congruence ratings differ so much between the two conditions of country residence? I interpret this result as an indication of personality changes among immigrants that escaped the notice of the brother or sister remaining in the home country. Again, those changes were most substantial for conscientiousness.

All these results reflect Polish immigrants in Western Europe. Perhaps they are peculiar to one national group? Findings from Study #3 (Boski, 2013, 2022) add some variability to this pattern. Here, we compared Ukrainian and Vietnamese immigrants, finding the latter group to outscore local Poles and East European peers in declared workload (hours per week) and self-assessed diligence. It may be that some cultures (e.g., post-Confucius East Asia) predispose their members to economic migration lifestyles more than others. Similarly, it is conceivable that migrants from other destinations may satisfy themselves with a less laborious lifestyle, counting on the social security support system.

2.2.3 Thrift, Savings, and Remittances

T_8. Thrift, savings, and remittances. Money earned through immigrants' hard work is likely not sufficient to cover all the needs and expectations of the family split between the home and host countries. Thrift and saving accompany effort as a complementary aspect of hard-work.

A bipolar scale of *Thrift – Extravagance* was constructed to measure this phenomenon (Boski, 2013). Participants were asked whether they would consider spending an extra 50€ monthly in purchasing thirteen categories of goods/ services to make life more comfortable or would judge such expenses as a *waste of money*. Immigrants proved more thrifty than Poles in the same income range, and Vietnamese were more thrifty than Ukrainians.

Remittances constitute the most important part of T_8. It remains as much a current economic phenomenon as it was in the past. Perhaps the earliest documentation of monetary transfers from immigrants comes from Thomas and Znaniecki (1918–20). In their *Polish Peasant in Europe and America*, we read about requests and acknowledgments of money receipts. Usually, those were transfers of a few dollars, sufficient for farm and life improvements back in local villages, which were reported in the letters sent to the overseas benefactors.

The evidence of immigrants' monetary transfers to their home countries comes from current economic analyses, not from psychological studies. According to World Bank data from 2017, the total of remittances during that year was $625 billion, an amount that exceeded Poland's GDP for that year.[8] From the difference between the outgoing and incoming flows of remittances, we can infer a lot about a country's economic and migratory status. For example, in 2017, outgoing remittances from the United States were $148.5 billion and incoming

---

[8] www.pewresearch.org/global/interactives/remittance-flows-by-country.

transfers were only \$6.6 billion. India (\$69 billion) and China (\$64 billion) were the two largest beneficiaries of remittances, with the Philippines, Mexico, Nigeria, Pakistan, Egypt, Vietnam, and Bangladesh next in line.

All of these leading beneficiaries are densely populated countries (with half of the world's population) in which large fractions of the people become economic migrants. There is a cultural–psychological explanation for the economic phenomena of immigrant remittances: the top beneficiaries are also the leading countries in family (in-group) collectivism (House et al., 2004), where helping the extended family is a matter of group solidarity and moral duty. All in all, the psychological mechanism explaining remittances at the individual and macro levels by the cultural dimension of family collectivism is a missing link in a process that starts with immigrants' hard work and thrift.

2.2.4 Lifestyles and Life Satisfaction

T_9. Psychological disharmony: Homo economicus, non-acculturation lifestyle.

This theorem introduces the concept of the psychological dimension of *harmony–disharmony*. Harmony reflects the idea of balanced domain activities around which individual life revolves. In childhood and adolescence, three such domains dominate: school, home/family life, and off-school peer contacts. In adult life, people attempt to reach a balance between work, family/children, and a variety of free-time social activities in associations that they join. There may be temporal disturbances in a harmonious lifestyle (e.g., students' exams, job search, childbirth), but they usually level out over a longer stretch of time. Immigration is a prolonged period whereby the previous psychological harmony is becoming shattered and a new one is still far from reach. Impermanence, including often-changed residences and workplaces, may characterize early periods of immigration, and occasional social contacts may replace stable relationships.

In Study #1, described under T_7, we received relevant information on this theme. The observers who rated the targets' personalities also provided us with information about the quality of interpersonal contact with those colleagues. A scale of interpersonal closeness was constructed of items measuring their joint off-work activities and emotional support. All five IPIP target-attributed personality traits were predictive of interpersonal closeness: four of them were positive, while conscientiousness was a single negative predictor (Boski, 2013; 2022, ch. 13). The last result carries an important theoretical load. Conscientiousness, an essential component of economic migrants' hard-working lifestyle, becomes at the same time an impediment to entering closer interpersonal contact with local people, which is essential for acculturation.

T_10. Life satisfaction and its components. Subjective well-being (as measured by the popular Satisfaction with Life Scale [SWLS] [Diener et al., 1985] or Cantril's Ladder) is often used in CCP as the outcome variable. This also applies to migration research. Still, because of the general outlook of these scales, we have constructed more specific measures of satisfaction with work and its outcomes: (i) Eudaimonia is intrinsic work satisfaction and anticipated goal attainment (*With my work, I am acquiring a valuable experience I will discount later*). (ii) Hedonism is pleasure with no reference to the future (*I do my best to make leisure time most pleasurable and relaxing for me*). (iii) Self-sacrifice is working at a repulsive job with a rewarding salary (*It is not important what kind of job you perform, but how much you are paid*). (iv) Alienation is disliking the job and its outcomes (*The time devoted to my work is wasted*). These four scales have very good internal reliabilities, although eudaimonia and alienation are largely mirror images of each other.

Because of intensive effort in performing jobs that were not freely chosen but taken of economic necessity, we hypothesized that self-sacrifice would be the essential life satisfaction component among economic immigrants. This hypothesis was not confirmed in our studies; surprisingly, eudaimonia prevailed as a more positive version of work and outcome evaluation.

Yet other findings, bridging changes in conscientiousness with lifestyle satisfaction accompanying immigrants' work, are worth reporting. As seen in Figure 4b, these relationships depend on the temporal orientation set in measuring the self-perceived changes. When in the prospective orientation, more conscientious immigrants experience eudaimonia in their current work and their level of alienation is low. On the contrary, the more conscientious immigrants were in retrospection before leaving Poland, compared to the present situation, the more their current job was accompanied by self-sacrifice and alienation. So it seems psychologically beneficial to immigrants' current adaptation if their predeparture life was deficient in work accomplishment.

2.2.5 Is There Anything Cultural in the Psychology of Economic Migrations?

The psychological approach to migration in the format just presented has been practiced neither in cross-cultural nor in cultural psychology. If anything, similar themes may be found in other social sciences under the theme of migration studies. Migrants' presence in the labor market in host countries and their remittances are of interest to economists. Their impact on the landscape of big cities in receiving countries raises the concern of social geographers, urban planners, and all who work in the area of multiculturalism (Boski, 2023). I have decided to cover the emerging subdiscipline of the psychology of economic migration in this Element in order to clear the ensuing presentation of acculturation from the EARN factors considered extraneous to LEARN.

Another reason for this inclusion is culture-specific. Successive waves of economic migrations have shaped the history of Poland since the end of the eighteenth century. Parallel to them were important achievements in literature, theatre, and film by artists who had been emigrants too. Their masterpieces form the foundations of contemporary school curricula in national literature and history. A striking common denominator of these works of art is their unanimously negative evaluation of economic emigration where the end result looms as a disaster of **self-dehumanization** (Boski, 2022). This artistic transformation of migratory *raw experience* can justifiably be named meta-cultural.

Economic migration and acculturation are both long-term processes with a growing overlap in later stages. For an economic migrant and his/her family, the process may end with a return to the homeland or it may become a permanent existence (Boski, 2010). In the latter case, it is more likely that it will be supplemented with an acculturation component, particularly pronounced with their second-generation offspring.

3 The Berry–Ward Model of Acculturation Attitudes

For the past forty years or so, the field of acculturation has been dominated by John Berry's model of acculturative attitudes (Berry, 1985, 2003, 2019; Berry et al., 2006). The model has become popular and is applied in the studies of numerous followers; at the same time, it has also been criticized on theoretical and psychometric grounds (e.g., Boski, 2008, 2022; Chirkov, 2009; Rudmin, 2003). Whatever one's theoretical position, it would be difficult to introduce a novel approach without first referring to that work.

Over decades, Berry has consistently quoted two definitions of acculturation, both worn out and lacking precision. According to Redfield and colleagues (1936), acculturation "comprehends those phenomena which result when groups of individuals having different cultures come into continuous first-hand contact, with subsequent changes in the original culture patterns of either or both groups" (p. 149). Another textbook formulation comes from Graves (1967), framed as a "psychological definition of acculturation" but also as an anthropological, community-level phenomenon. Here, the concept refers to changes in an individual participating in cultural contact, influenced both directly by the external culture and by the changing culture of which he/she is a member.

These two "classical definitions" lack clarity and precision; they appeared in texts that were not treatises but short articles of secondary importance. It is astounding that over the decades the leading author has not proposed a new definition of his own, serving the burgeoning field of research to which he largely has contributed. It is interesting that in his operationalizations of acculturation (i.e., scales), Berry does not include "psychological change," which both early formulations emphasized. I will now raise four major criticisms of Berry's model before finishing that review on a more positive note.

3.1 A Framework, Not a Theory of Acculturation

Granted the popularity of Berry's work, this heading may appear surprising. Yet this is aligned with the author's numerous writings in which he has never used the term "theory" but the much less restrictive "framework" (Berry, 1997, 2003, 2019). A framework is a collection of interconnected variables grouped in clusters.

The framework under scrutiny starts with population-level characteristics of cultures in contact and ends up with adaptation outcomes: psychological well-being and sociocultural adaptation, introduced by Colleen Ward (Ward, 2001; Ward & Rana-Deuba, 1999; Ward, Bochner & Furnham, 2001). However, the centerpiece of the framework is four *acculturation attitudes* (integration, assimilation, separation, and marginalization) that have been measured practically in any study conducted within Berry's approach.

Berry has sometimes referred to "strategies" as a proxy term for "attitudes." In his contribution to this Elements series (Berry, 2019), the term "strategies" appears eighty-six times (while "attitudes" appears thirty-four times); but that commonly used term was neither defined nor measured. In psychology, "strategies" are conceived as action programs designed to solve problems, to reach the desired goal, or to avoid misfortune. I have never encountered any research example of acculturation strategies understood this way; to the contrary, it is economic migrants who often develop intricate business or job search strategies before or after their settlement in the host country.

This point of discussion may be likened to an imagined situation in medicine in which health attitudes are substituted for objective health diagnoses. The intention is not to deny the importance of measuring attitudes and practicing a pro-health lifestyle, but to separate them from the "pure" medicine of testing and treatment. This comparison is relevant to our subject matter. In the approach I will present later, acculturation is about competencies in the second acquired culture, and about a bicultural configuration, which is very different from attitudes. **Competencies are not preferences, nor do preferences make competencies.**

In a broader scope, this distinction is fundamental for theoretical psychology and for empirical measures where objective tests are contrasted with subjective questionnaires. As the author of the eco-cultural model, Berry (1976, 1979, 2019) has been a champion of using objective measures of field (in)dependence associated with different subsistence ecological niches around the world. Yet this approach has been conceptually and empirically abandoned in acculturation studies by limiting the scope of research to subjective attitudes regarding the simultaneous retention of one culture (usually that of origin) and acquisition of another (usually that of the host country).

My position on this issue is exactly the opposite. Just as measuring people's attitudes about psychological differentiation would not push forward our understanding of eco-cultural adaptation, so acculturation should be conceived of and measured as a set of competencies in two (or more) cultural systems and not exclusively as attitudes. Attitudes may be useful in predicting behavior, but never at the expense of objective behavioral facts or competencies.

Next, attitudes have specified targets, be it an object (e.g., to purchase), a person or a party (e.g., to vote for), or a behavior (e.g., purchasing or voting). Attitudinal targets may be concrete (e.g., type of wine or detergent) or abstract (e.g., psychology or Platonian philosophy). But even in the latter case, the researcher would design one scale, rather than four as in Berry's case of acculturation. The most advantageous interpretation of his 2 x 2 box would be to regard the four constructs (integration, assimilation, separation, and marginalization [I, A, S, M]) as different personalized lifestyles in a new country, to be rated preferentially. Finally, if acquisition of a second culture is central to the concept of acculturation (which is my position), then the term "styles of life" seems more appropriate than "acculturation attitudes." Separation and marginalization – in Berry's terms – are explicit denials of the acquisition of a second culture. Altogether, Berry's acculturative framework is a loose collection of variables mapping the field of research; acculturative attitudes suffer from conceptual ambiguities as well as measurement problems, which will be illustrated in what follows.

3.2 Double-Barreled Ipsative Questions

Since the 1980s (e.g., Berry et al., 1989), through the International Comparative Study of Ethnocultural Youth (ICSEY) (Berry et al., 2006), until the most recent Mutual Intercultural Relations in Plural Societies (MIRIPS) project (Berry, 2018), Berry has propagated a research strategy in which attitude or preference items have been prepared in packages of four, corresponding to the dichotomized Yes/No two-country cross-section. This method of questionnaire construction has been criticized by Rudmin (2003, 2009) for violating the principles of item independence (or committing the error of ipsativity).

Here is an example of a quadruple item from MIRIPS.

- I: *It is important for me to be fluent in both [national language] and [ethnic language].*[9]
- A: *It is more important for me to be fluent in [national language] than in [ethnic language].*
- S: *It is more important for me to be fluent in [ethnic language] than in [national language].*
- M: *It is not important to me to be fluent in [ethnic language] or in [national language].*

Such item formulations are called *double-barreled questions* and they run against the fundamentals of questionnaire construction: never double – always a single item for a single problem. As Rudmin (2003) rightly observed, these are ipsative items, which means they lack a priori independence. Affirmative selection of one precludes a positive answer to any of the remaining three. Thus such items are destined to be negatively intercorrelated by the power of logic and are not psychometrically fit for any study. Despite this undeniable methodological argument, these faulty measures have remained intact over time, showing a broad range of intercorrelations, including highly positive ones.

To avoid the problem of ipsative measures, separate scales of home culture maintenance and host culture acquisition have also been proposed (e.g., Ryder et al., 2000; see also Celenk & Van de Vijver, 2011 for a review of these measures). Proceeding this way, the researcher will lose the opportunity of using four scales; at best he/she will end up with a typology resulting from a cross-section of two dimensions (by median or scale midpoint splits). Again, the main idea of four dimensions could be saved with the construction of vignettes/scenarios, which would personify the I, A, S, M scales and serve for preference ratings. Then the issue of ipsativity would not be an impediment.

3.3 Acultural Items, Content-Free Boxes

As we look at the examples of quadruple linguistic items, the recipe for scale construction appears extremely simple: *Use any two country labels of your choice, represented as [Nat = national, e.g., Canada] and [Eth = ethnic, e.g., Korea], and produce four options, resulting from their dichotomized [$_{Yes}$ NAT $_{No}$ | x [$_{Yes}$ ETH $_{No}$] cross-section. Select up to 10 life domains and create items by combining the dichotomized [Nat, Eth] sets of four with each of these domains. You will end up with 10 quadruple items, each contributing to four acculturation attitudes [I, A, S, M].*

---

[9] "National" refers to what is official or majoritarian in a country; "ethnic" refers to minorities or to immigrant groups.

This kind of instrument can be created in five to ten minutes. It is an automatized exercise and does not require the researcher to possess any cultural knowledge or competence. While language can often be identified by a single country label, other domains such as music, furniture, traditions, or social activities cannot.[10] Being him/herself ignorant, the researcher is not in a position to establish the sense and meaning that participants attach to these terms (e.g., Canadian music, Bolivian cuisine, Swiss traditions): is it valid and relevant, and does it objectively correspond to any cultural reality?

Moreover, cultural identity was approached and measured in a very similar way in the ICSEY (2006) and MIRIPS (2017) projects, with feelings attached to national and ethnic labels (groups and cultures).

Cultures are not equivalent to nation-states and their labels; they are much more complex entities. When group members and their heritage are reduced to such units (label → attributes), we are closer to their stereotyping than to cultural characteristics. For example, it would be meaningless and erroneous to use ethnic and national labels corresponding to Mozambican immigrants settling down in Kazakhstan. Home and host country in this scenario are complex and plural entities; neither of them has a single official language, and global English will likely be used for communication, if any occurs. So we need a flexible, multifaceted approach to cultures, not fixed-label tags as they appear in Berry-type questionnaires.

3.4 Integration on Top of Other Attitudes

Lack of realism manifests itself as a gap between acculturative attitudes and facts: *preferences are not competencies*. This catchphrase requires more elaboration here.

In Berry-style studies, integration (the double yes for home-ethnic and host-national cultures) has been consistently rated as the most favorable attitude/preference. It usually shows a ceiling effect, while the three remaining are below the midpoint of the scale (often a two-point difference on a five point scale). In their recent review and meta-analysis, Bierwiaczonek and Kunst (2021) note: "Across those samples for which we could obtain information on acculturation strategies, 69.45% of the participants were categorized as integrated, 9.60% as assimilated, 17.18% as separated, and 3.73% as marginalized" (p. 1486).

As a preference, integration carries high social approval: it sounds good to be generally positive to people and groups, whoever they are. Also, integration is attractive, doubling the benefits of both cultural worlds: it is advantageous to

---

[10] This is not the case in African countries, where "national" means formerly colonial, not derived from the name of the country.

speak two languages rather than only one, to have friends here and there, and to belong to two or more cultural worlds in general.

The problem is that groups that should score differently on integration measures in order to meet validity criteria do not show that. Rudmin (2003) used data collected initially by Kim (1988), who had studied acculturation attitudes among three categories of Koreans: (i) immigrants who settled in Canada; (ii) those with immigrant visas, preparing for relocation; and (iii) citizens of South Korea, uninterested in migration to Canada. The scores of these groups in four attitudes did not differ, with integration largely surpassing the three other scales. Rudmin added a fourth, fictitious category of "Norwegians in Norway imagining to be Koreans in Canada." Again, the pattern of results was identical to that of the three former groups, justifying the statement that integration is not necessarily related to acculturation but is representative of preferential social judgments in matters of international migration. Being equal for real and hypothetical immigrants, such measures cannot serve as effective predictors of real acculturative behaviors.

It should be recalled that although preferentially easy to affirm, integration is hard to accomplish as smooth bicultural functioning. Bilingual and normative behavioral fluency requires time and effort. At times, cultural patterns (belief systems, norms) contradict each other and make their harmonious joint practice impossible. In her analyses, Doucerain (2019, 2021) found the initial mental cost of integration much higher than that of a monocultural lifestyle. Benefits of a bicultural life may appear later when newly acquired competencies start paying off. But this road from preferences to competencies may be long and rough.

When we consider marginalization as the opposite of integration, it can hardly be imagined as a preferred orientation. But we can quite realistically see it as an outcome experienced by disfavored groups, particularly Indigenous people such as First Nations in North America, Australia, or Russian Eastern Siberia. There, the otherwise unthinkable situation of losing one's heritage culture while not acquiring that brought by the colonizers became the miserable reality.[11]

With assimilation, on the other hand, the lack of realism resides in ignoring the psychological makeup of adolescents or young adults, who usually form the large majority of immigrants. Such people cannot freely shed the culture of origin and replace it with that of the host country. Their programming in the culture of origin is a psychological datum; it may evolve but not be washed off.

---

[11] The plight of the First Nations' children, separated from their families and forced to live in church boarding schools, shocked Canada when the 150th anniversary of statehood was celebrated in 2017. The report on those tragic events, covering most of the twentieth century, is the best documentation of marginalization I have read (Gierak-Onoszko, 2019).

3.5 The Integration Hypothesis: How Solid Is Its Empirical Support?

Regardless of all of these systematically outlined criticisms, essential in Berry's acculturation framework is the **integration hypothesis**, which predicts that compared with those maintaining single culture preferences, migrants holding positive attitudes about home and host cultures enjoy superior psychological and sociocultural adaptation (the two criteria proposed by Colleen Ward). In a broader sense, integration is regarded as the most constructive outcome for living together in a pluralistic society. Since many studies applying Berry's paradigm have been accumulated over the years, they have provided material for meta-analyses to test the validity of the hypothesized relation.

First, a large meta-analysis (based on a sample of eighty-three studies) was published by Nguyen and Benet-Martinez (2013). They reported a large mean effect size of $r = 0.51$ when testing a random effects option (compared to a much smaller $r = 0.10$ for fixed effects). That result came as confirmation of the integration hypothesis. More recently, however, Bierwiaczonek and Kunst (2021) repeated Nguyen and Benet-Martinez's original meta-analysis, adding more samples from longitudinal studies. They used a different method to estimate effect sizes and arrived at a different conclusion: "Only 0.8% to 1.4% of the variance in adaptation was explained by acculturation, and the heterogeneity of these effects suggested that they were not only weak but also highly unstable" (p. 1480). With Berry and his colleagues currently coming out with new, multilevel meta-analyses of their data and employing different moderators for within- and between-country levels (e.g., progress in multicultural policies practiced by host countries or immigrants' religious denomination), the effect sizes favoring integration hypothesis are set at the modest level of $r \approx 0.15$ (Grigoryev et al., 2023).

All in all, we can conclude that the hypothesis bridging bicultural preferences with psychologically beneficial effects is likely, but it has not reached the status of a law of acculturation. Advancements in meta-analytical procedures combined with acculturation measures freed from the flaws discussed in this section may improve the precision of the integration hypothesis. Yet another way out from current incertitude is to search for another theoretical paradigm for acculturation. An attempt in this direction will be done in the next section of this Element.

4 A Three-Component Model of Acculturation

I started to work on my model of acculturation in 1984. It happened upon my arrival to Canada as a landed immigrant, in collaboration with John Berry, who invited and introduced me to the new field of research he had initiated not long before. Our daily contacts and academic discussions with John's doctoral students, Uichol Kim and Floyd Rudmin, were marked by a creative atmosphere, for which I feel indebted. Yet, already during that initial period, I sensed more reluctance than enthusiasm for exploring the field with the acculturation framework proposed by the mentor. Forty years ago, when preparing a pilot for what later became my first work on Polish immigrants in Canada (Boski, 1988b), I took a different approach. Knowledge and attachment to cultural symbols, and identities based on values shared with prototypical characters in both societies became the center of my interest. Over the years, the grains of those initial ideas were developed to form a theoretical model that I present today in its advanced format.

Three concepts elaborated earlier in this Element will serve as foundation blocks: (i) Cultural psychology provides its theoretical underpinnings. (ii) Second culture learning is its central theme. (iii) Competencies and biculturality are its outcomes. I will start with general conceptual issues and then move to the stage model, interspersed with empirical findings.

4.1 Conceptual Issues

4.1.1 First and Second Culture Learning/Acquisition: Three Layers of Culture

Acculturation psychology has surprisingly ignored the process of first culture acquisition/learning, which is usually called *enculturation* (Berry et al., 2011, p. 13; Matsumoto & Juang, 2004, p. 134). Although enculturation is a textbook concept, it is not explained there with sufficient clarity, and it does not appear in thematic proximity to acculturation. Moreover, it would be hard to question the validity of the statement: "Enculturation is rarely studied by culturally oriented psychologists." A comparative analysis of both processes is as much needed as it is missing. Steps in this direction will be made in this section. Individuals functioning as members of any culture are programmed by its three layers: **language – symbols – values/practices**. This simple model is presented in Figure 5.

Both processes – enculturation and acculturation – occur through (i) culturalization, which covers intentional instruction, and (ii) socialization, which refers to incidental acquisition.[12] The three layers are interconnected but retain relative autonomy. The dotted diagonal line across the circle represents the proportion to which each layer is subject to culturalizing instruction and practical socialization (apprenticeship).

---

[12] The term "culturalization" is borrowed from Kłoskowska (2000/1996): "Entering the symbolic culture universe, including that of national culture is what is meant by culturalization" (p. 109).

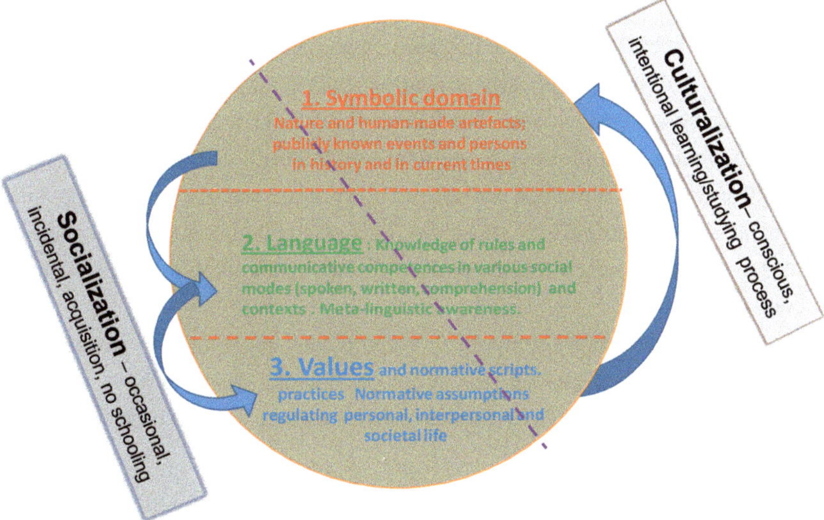

Figure 5 Three layers of culture in enculturation and acculturation research

Symbolic Layer

I have borrowed the concept of symbolic culture from Antonina Kłoskowska (2000/ 1996), a Polish sociologist of culture. "Nation [. . .] is a commonality of autotelic values and symbols whereby these values find their expression [. . .] National culture opens a space for symbolic communication" (p. 109). It covers all historical and current events considered important for citizens in a country to form their knowledge and guide them across daily life activities. Its elements consist of nature-shaped and human-made artifacts: sacred places and revered monuments; honored dates commemorated as important anniversaries; religious and secular holidays or festivals; and public figures, historic and contemporary heroes, celebrities, famous artists, sports champions, and other iconic objects of the culture.

Symbolic space covers the public area of the whole country, its regions, and cities, together with the natural environment, forming a rich and meaningful eco-cultural niche. In their material substance, symbols are often visual stimuli – images, pictures, sculptures, and monuments – but equally, they may take auditory form, appearing as anthems, hymns, classic and popular music, and songs.

Ritualistic celebrations are elicited by and take place around these symbols. People know their meaning and the proper behaviors they are expected to enact on special occasions (Cole, 1995, 1996). Thus symbols are formative to cultural identity and are used to activate it (Chen et al., 2008; Hong et al., 2000). It is suggested in Figure 5 that symbolic learning occurs mainly through culturalization – that is, during formal instruction at school or other occasions of intentional teaching (e.g., visits to *must-see* places).

Language

Humans do not exist outside the linguistic space of their culture. The paradox is that so little is done theoretically and empirically on this fundamental aspect of our psychological endowment. The basics of our first language are acquired as part of the maturation process in interaction with family members. Since school instruction became universal about a century ago, literacy in the first/native tongue attained a compulsory status too. This is why language, in our scheme, is split into approximately equal proportions between spontaneous acquisition and school instruction.

Because the linguistic component accompanies most of our psychological processes, it is also present in the symbolic domain. Words may complement pictorial or auditory symbols by enriching their meaning (e.g., as lyrics in songs).[13]

Cultural Values and Practices

Values and practices are the key elements of enculturation and they pervade all research questionnaires in the field of CCP. Unlike Berry–Ward-style instruments that are framed in a broad, content-free way, (e.g., Canadian [national] vs. Korean [ethnic] traditions), the axio-normative elements in my approach are culture-specific and contextual (e.g., *addressing university lecturers by first names rather than by academic title*).

Compared to the other two layers, cultural values and practices are rarely the subject of school instruction, which is illustrated in Figure 5 by the small fraction of its third layer on the culturalization side. Appropriate or inappropriate behavior is a matter of – telling/showing "how to do it?"; commenting, and rewarding or punishing. Children do not receive explanations for why they should obey elders, or – in reverse – express and retain their autonomous judgments. In each case, "it is the proper thing to do."

It is assumed that on reaching maturity, a young adult has acquired sufficient cognitive and behavioral competencies in all three layers of national culture to function as an enculturated citizen of his/her country. Today, it becomes more or less equivalent to a secondary school diploma. As with each domain of human endeavor, there are different levels of competence: from experts to individuals suffering deficiencies in cognitive skills (knowledge, communication illiterates) and social behavior (unsocialized criminals). The latter categories occupy the lowest rungs in the societal hierarchy as unskilled workers or inmates.

---

[13] The symbolic and linguistic components of culture learning are closely related; still, they retain a relative autonomy. The split is clear when the official and native tongue is of historically foreign origin while the nation-state has been independent, building its own identity. Also, immigrants or natives residing outside the home country may use the first language for communication purposes but remain unfamiliar with the symbols of current events.

4.1.2 From Enculturation to Acculturation

An individual who learns her/his maternal culture and another person for whom it becomes a second culture both face the same three layers. Still, the processes and outcomes of enculturation and acculturation differ; the passage is illustrated in Figure 6.

Comparing Enculturation and Acculturation

1. *The time factor.* Enculturation is about parental or first culture (C1) acquisition. There are rare cases of simultaneous acquisition of maternal and paternal cultures in mixed families when the two processes are not differentiated in time. Apart from these rare situations, acculturation follows enculturation in a wide range of possible time intervals. Each of the three layers in C1 forms a baseline and is responsible for transfer conditions that interfere with C2 learning/acquisition.

2. *Conditions for enculturation and acculturation.* (i) In each society there is a systematically organized period for enculturation: schooling and/or apprenticeship for a new generation to acquire the necessary skills to function as adult citizens. The culturalization and socialization aspects are harmoniously combined. (ii) Contrariwise, acculturation is much less systematic, and it occurs in two largely different sets of conditions:

   - Second language/culture schooling as part of a nonmigratory C1 educational system. (This also includes additional, private courses organized by parents for their children.) It is predominantly a culturalization process with little practical application.

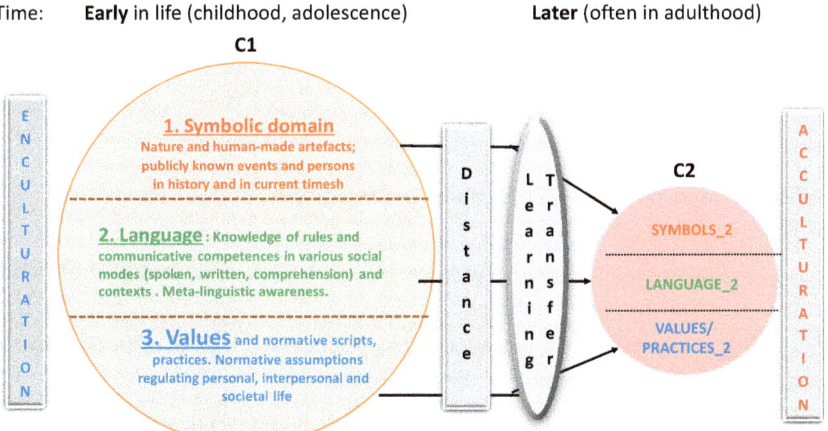

Figure 6 From C1 = Enculturation to C2 = Acculturation

- On-the-job, practical C2 acquisition, which happens mainly to adult immigrants who do not manifest willingness to devote their time, energy, and money to learn the culture of their sojourn or settlement.

3. *Across generations*. As a consequence of 1 and 2, the profiles of enculturation and acculturation outcomes may vary largely from person to person, but C1 competence levels in all three layers should prevail over the corresponding C2 layers. The order of C1 and C2 becomes reversed across immigrant generations. For second-generation children who attend host culture schools, their parental culture of origin may become secondary and the subject of acculturation. Negative transfer from being earlier programmed in C1 is the main mechanism for difficulties and deficits in C2 acculturation. Figure 6 illustrates this mechanism with a *transfer lens* positioned between C1 and C2, and responsible for their unequal sizes.

4. *Cultural dominance*. For these reasons, the native, C1 culture learned and acquired in enculturation becomes dominant in regulatory functions over the C2 culture, acquired later via acculturation.

Acculturation: Definition and Corollaries

Definition. Psychological acculturation is conceived as (i) a culture-learning process whereby new linguistic competencies, symbolic meanings, and values/ practices (ways of being), (ii) necessary for becoming a functional member of a receiving society, (iii) are gradually acquired through organized instruction and/or by one's effort, (iv) with or without prior migration, and (v) up to the limits set by former enculturation and the distance separating the two cultures, (vi) which create difficulties known as acculturative stress. (vii) Biculturality is the direction and outcome of this process (viii) when affective identities supplement cognitive and behavioral competencies.

Corollaries. This definition is complex but more precise than the classical formulae cited by Sam and Berry (2006) and by Berry (2019). Its main characteristics are:

- The second culture (C2) learning process superimposed on the first (C1) culture enculturation.
- The distance separating C1 and C2, which determines the levels of difficulty in skill acquisition and coherence.
- Objective competencies are measured by tests rather than self-rated preferences through questionnaires or inventories.
- Biculturalism is the distant goal of acquiring/maintaining competencies and identities.

- Affective factors such as acculturative stress, hassles, and psychological adjustment (life satisfaction and symptoms of maladaptation) are recognized, but not as definitional components. (They do not enter as components of enculturation either.)

- Acculturation is a long process in an individual's personal life and across generations. The length of time and the stage of the process are rarely specified in a particular study. Yet these characteristics are essential for the problems under investigation and the outcomes of such studies. In my handbook presentation (Boski, 2022, ch. 13), I articulated several sequential stages. Here they will be compressed into two: preliminary and advanced.

- This definition proposes biculturality as the outcome of the process. I am aware, in line with the conceptual work by Morris and his colleagues (Morris, Chiu & Liu, 2015), that biculturalism is a somehow simplified version of polyculturalism, which the authors consider more adequate for understanding humans in the twenty-first century. Still, all models and research designs in the field have accepted the bicultural perspective and I comply with it in this Element.

4.2 Model of Acculturation I: Early Stages

At early stages, the model outlines the situation of a newcomer entering a country that may be completely foreign for that person, arriving as a student-sojourner, an expatriate, or an immigrant (though the latter's

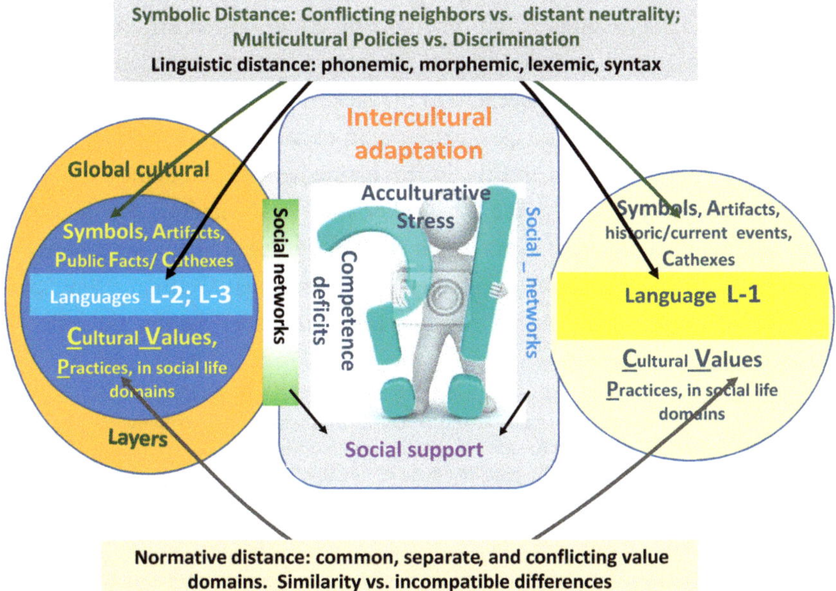

Figure 7 The model of acculturation I: Early stages

adaptation has been dealt with separately in two sections before). This model is illustrated in Figure 7.

Two circles on the sides of Figure 7 represent cultures C1 (home) and C2 (host/foreign) respectively, each sliced into three layers. Additionally, C2 is encircled by a global cultural layer reflecting the reality of living abroad with a third culture (nowadays usually Anglophone) as a common platform for communication between locals and newly arrived migrants. This is a typical situation for international students whose instruction will occur in English – that is, in a third language, neither of the home country nor of the host country (e.g., Turks in Poland).[14] Thus acculturation beyond the global linguistic regions (such as Anglo-, Spanish-, or Francophone countries) is a complex matter where to communicate, hosts and guests meet on a third, neutral platform (which is usually English). Four important elements characterize this preliminary phase of acculturation.

4.2.1 Cultural Distance

This is a concept that appears in many works on acculturation, but rarely in elaborated formats, and separately for the three culture components. The intuitive presumption is that large cultural distance is a hindrance to effective acculturation and a source of acculturative stress.

Linguistic distance. This is perhaps conceptually the most advanced of the three facets of distance. It can be divided into several subsystems corresponding to linguistic structures: phonological, morphological, syntax, and lexical (Kurcz, 2007). Consequently, all others being equal, group differences in L2 competencies depend on that distance. Departure from the standards of native speakers occurs at all levels because of the lack of correspondence between the subsystems of the two languages, resulting in negative transfer from L1 to L2 (Grosjean, 1997). This is mostly heard in inadequate phonemes – that is, a *foreign accent* that betrays the L2 speaker. Similar difficulties and inadequacies occur in the domain of syntax. The lack of articles in Slavic languages, for example, makes the task of using them in Roman and Germanic languages an objective challenge. On the reverse side, Slavic languages are inflected

---

[14] Here we have a situation that is unknown to researchers and practitioners in main Anglophone countries, where sojourners come having acquired some skills, measured by the Test of English as a Foreign Language (TOEFL), enabling them to function in that language in most domains of their lives. Almost all students from Africa, Asia, or Latin America whom I have met, talked with, or interviewed, reported zero knowledge about Poland when they decided to accept the admission and travel to that country. Literally, it meant for them inability of locating this country on the world map. A similar situation occurs with many other countries that do not belong to the category of main migration destinations.

languages, which creates hurdles for Westerners in using correct noun and adjective declension.

Symbolic distance. It appears as ignorance of the other culture and/or as an opposite appraisal of historical and contemporary figures, events, and the like. Lack of historical contacts results in mutual ignorance, and historical conflicts are commemorated in different ways across the border. It is not a random circumstance that Gare d'Austerlitz is a railway station in Paris while Waterloo Station is in London. Symbolic distance between cultures C1 and C2 may not be symmetrical. Often one of them is more dominant on the global stage, and in this sense, it becomes cognitively more available which is particularly the case of the global cultural layer.

Values and their practical manifestations in behavioral scripts. The third facet of cultural distance is normative. During the first stages of cultural contact, inherent differences take the form of visible public behaviors, such as the way people dress, smile, or show politeness. People visiting Poland observe a low frequency of smiling on the streets, and Polish immigrants notice more smiling in Western countries (see Hekiert, 2018 and Kryś et al., 2014 on cross-cultural differences in smiling frequency).

Counterintuitively, we have learned from the investigations conducted with Erasmus exchange students that large cultural distances may be desirable and attractive in places reaching high scores on dimensions positively associated with *civilization advancement.* Thus, when the host country/university exceeds the home country or institution on GLOBE's performance orientation, future orientation, and orderliness (high uncertainty avoidance) (House et al., 2004), students experience high levels of satisfaction with their sojourn (Boski, 2022, ch. 13; Więckowska, 2012).

4.2.2 Affective Honeymoon and Acculturative Stress

Affective aspects of acculturation have attracted researchers' attention from the earliest studies in the middle of the twentieth century (Lysgaard, 1955; see also Hofstede, 2001, p. 426). There, we were led to believe that the early stage of cultural contact, euphemistically called the honeymoon, was generally positive and marked by blissful states.

Acculturative stress (or shock) has a central place in Colleen Ward's (2001) and in John Berry's (2006, 2019) models. Ward and her colleagues (2001) spent much time discussing various shapes of stress curves along the time dimension (e.g., *inverted U, J,* or *W*). There are no convincing arguments to expect a general law linking the sojourn's length of time with the intensity of affective responses of new arrivals. Sojourners, when coming as invited visitors and greeted with hospitality programs, may enjoy this "honeymoon," as was the case with the Fulbright fellows in Lysgaard's study. But the experiences of such categories of migrants cannot be generalized to all others, who start their new life in very different circumstances. In my studies on Polish immigrants in the United States, those of the first generation were compared with peers born and raised in America (from Polish parents). Life satisfaction scores on Cantril's Ladder were anchored in five points of their lifetime, starting from their childhood, until the present time and five years in the future. The main result was a deep dip in young immigrants' subjective well-being at the time of arrival, compared to their premigration lives and their second-generation peers of the same age when leaving family homes and starting independent lives (Boski, 1992, 2022).

I find the treatment of acculturative stress or culture shock in some approaches (e.g., Ward, Bochner & Furnham, 2001) as overemphasized. As our definition specifies, stress is a factor accompanying acculturation to varying degrees, but should not be regarded as its essence.[15] Another problem is that the concept has been used in acculturation research in a very broad sense, with measures concentrating on psychological symptoms (depression, anxiety, or psychosomatic symptoms), hassles, and everyday life difficulties. Control groups of local people are not used in such studies to determine whether immigrants score higher on these measures. Also, since the distinction between the psychology of economic immigration and acculturation is the major split proposed in this Element, problems with finding and securing jobs or with coping with fatigue and unemployment are not our focus. Like cultural distance, acculturative stress has three specific facets: linguistic, symbolic, and normative.

- Linguistic stress appears in any public situation when the migrant's/sojourner's performance depends on his/her speech production or comprehension.
- Symbolic stress may be less disturbing in day-to-day activities, but it appears as an uncomfortable ignorance on special occasions or celebrations, and as possible boredom or loneliness when locals actively pursue their rituals and experience cultural identity. Felt prejudice, as an important source of stress, also belongs here.
- Normative stress is a consequence of inconsistent or antagonistic expectations regarding desirable conduct in home and host cultures.

---

[15] Interestingly, since Freud's era, the stress of enculturation has not been discussed in the literature, even though its presence cannot be denied (e.g., in toilet training).

4.2.3 Acculturative Stress in Second Language Use and during the Covid-19 Epidemic

The concept of visible minorities is used in the literature on prejudice. A linguistic minority may be of equal importance when the way people speak a second language betrays their origin, which they might otherwise like to disguise. In the past, speaking Polish with a Russian or Ukrainian accent fell into this category.[16] Hrysha (2016) studied these phenomena among Ukrainian students in Poland: how were their linguistic competencies linked to anxiety and strategic self-presentation in public? She found that young Ukrainians were hiding their identity in two ways: (i) through demonstrating high competence in L2 (trying not to be recognizable as a foreign speaker); and (ii) by a defensive strategy of increased self-awareness, sensitivity to prejudice threat, and avoidance in social interactions.

Two of our recent studies were conducted in the context of the COVID-19 epidemic. Żywek (2021) compared contact quality and emotions of local and international students with Polish lecturers, colleagues, and university administration. The pre-COVID offline versus COVID online periods did not matter, but the quality of contact (e.g., level of communication, attention, understanding) with all three categories of interaction partners was enhanced among local Polish students compared to their international peers. Also, the emotional responses of the latter group to their interactants were more intensive (both in positive and in negative ways). These results may be interpreted as indicative of acculturative stress among international students compared to local students.

The other study (Darau, 2021) compared stress at work among French, *naturalisés* (French-educated former immigrants), and Romanian immigrant physicians during the COVID-19 pandemic in France. Conscientiousness, which was earlier discussed as a personality trait responsible for immigrants' hard work, now lowered their stress level, contrary to French physicians, whose conscientiousness resulted in enhanced stress at work (the moderation for French vs. immigrant physicians was significant, $p < 0.001$).

To summarize, not all sources of stress affecting immigrants should be regarded as acculturative. When it comes to such universally dramatic events as a pandemic, it is necessary to design studies with local control groups, comparing them with immigrants.

---

[16] I am referring to the times before the current Russian aggression against Ukraine, which brought millions of bilingual Ukrainian–Russian refugees to Poland who are treated in a friendly way.

4.2.4 Social Networks

Interactions with home- or host-individuals/groups and international sojourners are sources of information, learning, and emotional support. The issue of social networks was introduced in Section 2.

Studies on international students, often on short-term exchange programs, have explored the types of interpersonal relationships these young people enter during such sojourns (Biłas-Henne, 2009; Boski, 2022). The results of these studies bring a clear message, contradicting the notion of desirable expansion of intercultural horizons among young Europeans. The pre-sojourn expectations are to enter new relationships with the host and international colleagues. In reality, sojourners establish new bonds with their fellow compatriots and other international students (most often within the same cultural region – e.g., Scandinavian, Roman, or Slavic ethnolinguistic groups). The fewest contacts are reported with the local hosts, and they turn out to be the least rewarding. This appears as a universal tendency of in-group favoritism operating against the odds such as the low probability of finding a bird of a feather: finding compatriots is indeed difficult in some foreign universities, yet such individuals are actively sought.

The common living space for host locals and foreign sojourners is limited, while communication is effortful, in contrast with people who speak the same mother tongue. Nevertheless, those students who venture to establish contacts with local people report better adjustment and higher life satisfaction (Biłas-Henne, 2009; Biłas-Henne & Boski, 2014). These spontaneous group processes may be altered at universities by facilitating basic acculturation for international and local students together.[17]

4.3 Model of Acculturation II: Advanced Stages

I am passing now to the advanced stages of acculturation when a person proceeds toward acquiring bicultural competencies and becoming a bicultural individual. There appear to be structural changes between the elements depicted in the Stage I model (Figure 7) and the present model in Figure 8.

Acculturative stress is an element missing in the new model. This is not to say that a person in the process has been freed of difficulties with C2 or with establishing a harmonious relationship between both cultures. The point is that he/she knows how to handle them and is not confused or disorganized.

---

[17] We introduced such courses at SWPS University in Warsaw more than ten years ago. The English title was "Understanding Poland and Living among Poles" (a similar course has been also offered in Russian). "Understanding Poland" is focused on all three layers of culture as components of acculturation and enhances daily contacts with local people.

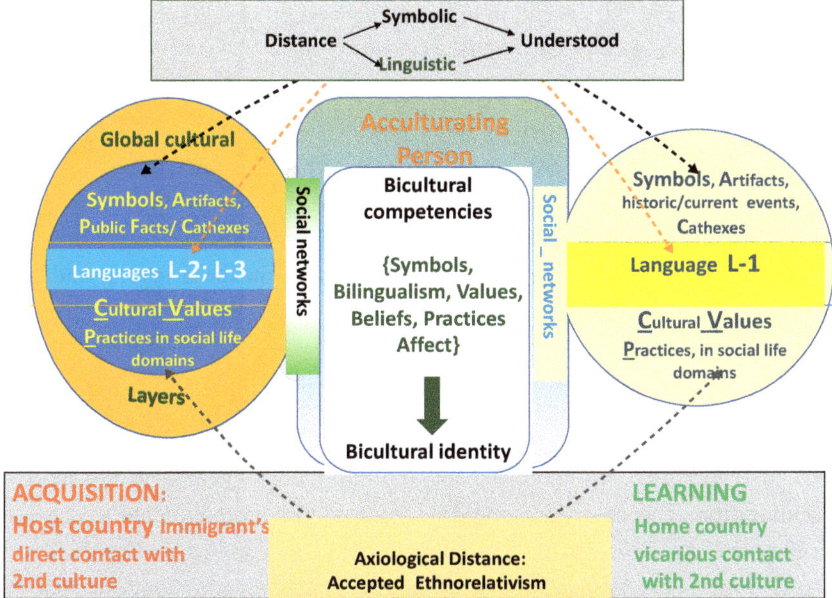

Figure 8 The model of acculturation II: Advanced stages

By the same token, subjectively felt cultural distance is lower (Boski, 1991, 1992), which can be seen in the dotted lines.

Also novel here is the distinction between migrant and sedentary types of acculturation. The latter is a remote type of learning and has been recognized by other authors as an alternative to migration.[18] Vicarious acculturation in the home country is a worldwide phenomenon, but we should note that studying foreign languages (or in foreign languages) is not a new phenomenon. It has characterized education in Europe since the Middle Ages. Latin was the language of educationally and socially privileged people; that later switched to French and, more recently, to English. Across centuries, a good education has been equated with cognitive acculturation.

These processes have intensified with globalization. Starting an L2 education at the preschool level is a new development practiced on a large scale in many countries (e.g., Poland). Education in international schools, elementary or high schools, and full-degree university studies in/of foreign language and culture can serve as a model for vicarious acculturation. This means an intensive immersion program with the presence of native speakers as teachers and all channels of intercultural exposure. English has become the *main second*

---

[18] Ferguson et al. (2020) discuss remote acculturation in the context of Jamaican youth vis-a-vis the US. Also Berry (2019) in his Element commented that a direct intercultural contact was not necessary for acculturation to occur.

language globally, but education in two foreign languages is standard in the EU (Boski, Kmiotek & Shatruk, 2020).

Although vicarious (or remote) acculturation is not a full-scale immersion in C2, and its philological component of school learning may dominate over *real-life* behavioral scripts, it is still an indispensable part of cultural learning.[19] Its obvious advantage is control over acculturative stress, which is limited to classroom situations and subordinate to positive motivation and interest. I will now present acculturation research in three layers, and later their interconnections.

4.3.1 Bilingualism and Multilingualism

In line with the overall perspective of this Element and the theoretical orientation just presented, bilingualism and multilingualism belong to the field of acculturation. This assertion should be conceptually as convincing as it is rare in practice. As Grosjean (2015; see also Ramírez-Esparza & García-Sierra, 2014) titled his essay "Bicultural Bilinguals," the juncture suggests that the two concepts may be overlapping but in a limited scope. Not so in my approach, where bilingualism is just a part of biculturalism.

In reality, what we observe makes even Grosjean's tacit attempt look bold: acculturation researchers do not study bilingualism and do not feel confident in this domain. If participants in acculturation studies are asked about their bilingual repertoire, it takes the form of subjective self-assessment and frequency of life situations where these languages are spoken. Such measures are largely insufficient. On the other side too, most psycholinguists constrain their interests to linguistic matters, isolating themselves from other layers of acculturation research. As a result, the field becomes deficient due to this split. The language-free approach to acculturation runs contrary to commonsense knowledge that proficiency in a second language is a condition for a successful life when abroad. To thrive as a scholarly discipline, acculturation psychology cannot afford to ignore the voices of the real world. The goal of this section is to take a step toward overcoming these inadequacies.

Literature on bilingualism may contribute to the psychology of acculturation in two ways. The first is linguistically oriented, with an emphasis on skill and information processing. The other has to do with language affecting other psychological processes and communication pragmatics. I will analyze them in this order.

---

[19] As no student pilot or cosmonaut will be sent on a real flight without previous training in simulation capsules, so more and more people start their intercultural life with vicarious acculturation practised within the context of the home country. This leaves millions of economic immigrants and refugees beyond such comfort zone.

Linguistic Approaches and Experimental Psycholinguistics

Here, competencies are assessed by objective tests measuring a variety of skills: phonemic, grammatical, vocabulary, text, speech comprehension, and speech fluency (Komorowska & Krajka, 2017). Two-way translation and oral comprehension are the popular methods practiced in foreign-language courses and certification exams. The measure of oral comprehension is useful only for L2 testing since it is only reasonable to assume that native speakers will have a perfect comprehension of everyday parlance. A different story concerns translation, which can be tested both ways. Here an interesting practice can be observed globally, that professional simultaneous translation, as well as in novels and poetry, is always executed by native speakers from the original in L2 to their L1.

These classical methods were applied in Kmiotek's (2020) dissertation (which will be referred to more in subsequent sections of this Element). Oral comprehension in Polish and French was tested in five groups: Polish university students of French language and culture (from Warsaw and Wrocław), first-generation Polish immigrants in France, and second-generation Polish youths attending high schools in Lyon and Brussels. There were no between-group differences in comprehension of the Polish language, but the level of French was considerably lower among university students who were in the process of vicarious acculturation. Most likely, limited exposure to L2 in academia is not sufficient for the comprehension of colloquial, everyday conversation between natives.

Experimental methods, often exploiting reaction times to words in L1 and L2 (as well as pseudo words) can also count as part of linguistically oriented research (Bialystok et al., 2009; Bialystok & Luk, 2012). Although there is a consensus about the psychological advantages of bilingualism, some costs are also pointed out. One of them is the prolonged reaction time bilinguals display in the classical Stroop effect. Agata Skiba (2016) applied this methodology in her study of Polish–Spanish bilinguals from Spain, Mexico, and Poland.[20] Polish monolinguals (not cognizant of Spanish) made up the third group. Color words in both languages appeared in two formats of visual ↔ semantic sets:

- compatible: red (czerwony, rojo), green (zielony, verde), blue (niebieski, azul), and black (czarny, negre); and
- incompatible: red (czerwony, rojo), black (czarny, negre), green (zielony, verde), and blue (niebieski, azul).

---

[20] Polish bilinguals were more balanced than Spanish bilinguals, as measured by their formal certificates and history of L2 learning. Poles learned Spanish at schools or university; native Spanish speakers acquired communicative skills in Poland during their sojourn in Poland (as Spanish-language teachers or expatriates).

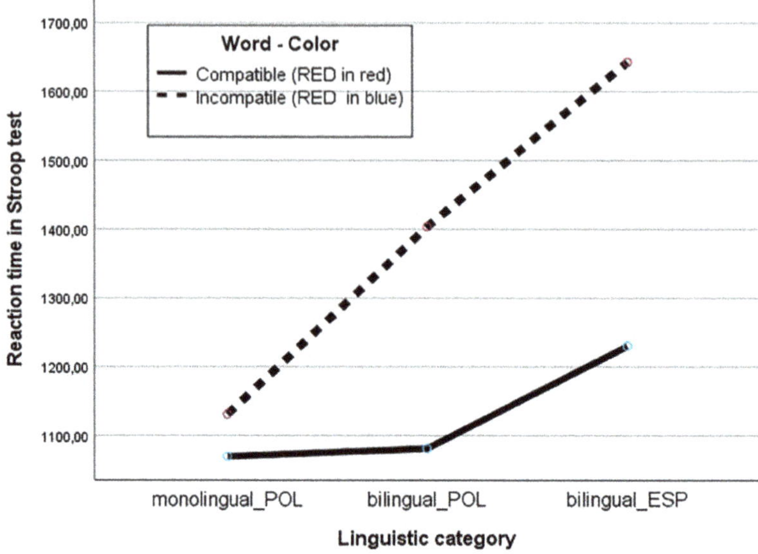

Figure 9 The Stroop effect among monolinguals and bilinguals (Skiba, 2016)

The standard task in this type of experiment was to answer "in which color is the word written" by clicking one of the letters (marked with an appropriately colored sticker) on a computer keyboard.

Results (see Figure 9) revealed a typical pattern of longer reaction times for incompatible words when the cognitive conflict between the visual and the semantic facets of the stimuli occurred. However, the gap between incompatible and compatible conditions was not significant among Polish monolinguals and it grew large in bilinguals from both countries (more substantial among Spanish bilinguals). Of all the experimental conditions, monolinguals, as Spanish illiterates, had the lowest reaction times for incompatible words in that language, not different from the compatible conditions (regardless of the language). This effect was accounted for by observing that since the semantic aspect of the *color words* was absent for these participants, the conflict with color perception was likewise absent. Incompatibility between the semantic and perceptual is not a suitable construct for monolinguals outside of their mother tongue.

The conclusions of this experiment can be generalized to explain important phenomena of bilingual processing and communication. Among these, a distinction between *coordinate, compound,* and *subordinate* types of bilingualism (Kurcz, 2000, 2007) is of theoretical relevance here. The *coordinate* version assumes two separate systems in each language: for words and corresponding concepts. In the *compound* version, one joint set of concepts serves two languages.

Finally, in the *subordinate* category, L2 concepts are accessed by L1. If we consider these three categories as lined up from the most (coordinate) to the least (subordinate) advanced, then coordinate bilinguals should not mix the two languages, and their reaction times in the Stroop experiment will not be impaired. Compound bilinguals may interject words from the rival language in their speech and experience cognitive conflict typical of the Stroop effect. Finally, the reaction times in subordinate bilinguals who search for proper words in L2 should be the longest.

This theory of bilingual levels of information processing may explain Skiba's experimental results: from the lowest reaction times among *monolinguals*, through medium reaction times among Polish *compound* speakers, and the highest among Spanish *subordinate* bilinguals.

Psychological Processes in L1 and L2: Emotions in Languages

The second approach is more psychological in the sense that the research questions probe how first (L1) and second (L2) languages affect outer linguistic functions (e.g., experience and expression of emotions). It has gradually been accepted that work on bilingualism cannot be reduced to a purely linguistic parallel translation between the L1 and L2 users. Of great contribution are the studies of Anna Wierzbicka (1994, 1999), who has become a champion in the literature, clearly demonstrating the limits of affective and general concept translatability between languages.

In her analyses, Wierzbicka uses not statistical tools but the power of semantic analyses by interpreting emotional codes in L1 when attempting their translation into L2. She offers an example, describing her experience when listening to recorded music she received from overseas:

> The thought I wanted to express was very clear in my mind, and it was the one which formed itself in Polish: *Słuchałam ze wzruszeniem* (*I listened with* . . .). But as I struggled to transfer this thought from Polish to English, I realized it was not possible to do so. The participle *wzruszony* can be translated to English as "moved" (*I was moved*). But it is not possible to say in English that one listened to some music with an emotion corresponding to the word "moved." (Wierzbicka, 2007, p. 97)

The author continued her attempts to find proper words in English for her *Polish-felt emotion* (e.g., *I listened to it with emotion, pleasure*), finding none of them suitable. The whole book *Translating Lives*, from which this quote was borrowed, was written by experts and bilingual scholars documenting similar barriers in other languages. One may say that while *crude* translations may be satisfactory for some purposes, authors like Wierzbicka emphasize what is *lost in translation* at a deeper level.

Research closer to the methodological rigors of psychology has been advanced by other authors, of whom I will refer mainly to Dewaele and Pavlenko (2003), who designed the Bilingualism and Emotions Questionnaire (BEQ), which provided them with a database that was exploited in many papers that followed. Dewaele, a prolific researcher on emotions felt and expressed by bilinguals, devoted much attention to studies on intensive emotional states negative (swear words) and positive (love).

In his earlier work, Dewaele (2008) found that the affective intensity of *I love you* was considered by bilinguals nearly two times stronger (45%: 25%) in their L1 than in their L2. (In some languages, notably East Asian languages, love is not expressed verbally, though.) Later, in a paper, "Loving a Partner in a Foreign Language" (Dewaele & Salomidou, 2017), the authors reminded the reader of a French play, *Cyrano de Bergerac*, where the main character (Christian) showed his ineptitude in expressing tender feelings to Roxanne in his poor L2, which was French, causing her linguistic disappointment. Thus the situation was similar to that Wierzbicka analyzed in her hesitation in finding an English equivalent of Polish words for feelings when listening to music. Referring to their empirical findings, Dewaele and Solomidou concluded that difficulty with *I love you* in L2 is an initial phenomenon that disappears as the relationship stabilizes with time.

Studies on swear words (Dewaele, 2004, 2010) have proven that bilinguals regarded those *bad words* as weaker and used them less frequently than the corresponding expressions in L1. Pavlenko (2012) summarized the results of many studies comparing emotionality ratings of affective words in L1 (when dominant) and L2 this way:

> To explain these effects, I have put forth a **theory of language embodiment** (Pavlenko, 2005) which sees affective socialization in early childhood as the process of integration of phonological forms of words and phrases with information from visual, auditory, olfactory, tactile, kinesthetic, and visceral modalities, autobiographical memories, and affect … This explanation, concerning foreign languages, commonly involves the **decontextualized** nature of the language classroom, which does not provide many opportunities for integration of all sensory modalities and verbal conditioning … and thus leads to the development of "**disembodied**" words, used freely by speakers who do not experience their full impact. (p. 421)[21]

---

[21] All bolds in the quote from Pavlenko (2012) are mine – PB.

The distinction between L1 *embodiment* and L2 *disembodiment* concerning the conditions of language learning/acquisition is particularly relevant for the theoretical model of acculturation presented in this Element. It fits very well with the contrast between the culturalization and socialization processes of the three layers of culture. Indeed, preschool children acquire their mother tongue largely in the sensory mode of cognition, which characterizes this stage of cognitive development in general (Pavlenko, 2004). Later, at school, this process is continued in a more neutral, "disembodied" way, but linguistic emotionality in L1, from which school education abstains, is not uprooted. The process is reversed in L2 learning at the school level; here, the emotional language, including swear words, is the last classroom expression to be learned (if at all). So, whenever they are acquired, they may miss the power of L1 equivalents.

When building their theory of linguistic (dis)embodiment, Dewaele and Pavlenko assumed a typical academic process of L2 learning. It may be a different story, though, when we consider immigrants for whom street life is *the school of language* and swear words heard in emotional situations may be among the first to be acquired. As a contribution to the line of studies transcending purely linguistic substance, I will present an investigation comparing conversational behaviors displayed by bilinguals in interactions carried out in their mother tongues and in their second language.

Gestures and Smiles in Bilingual Conversations (Polish–Turkish Study)

Classical studies on perilingual behaviors (gestures, smiles, gaze, physical distance to the partner of interaction) compared monocultural individuals from various ethnolinguistic groups (Hecht, Andersen & Ribeau, 1989). Our research problem was different: what kind of change in these conversation-accompanying behaviors will occur when bilingual individuals switch from their L1 to L2? Here, two lines of theoretical reasoning can be drawn. The first is based on the imbalance of linguistic competencies between L1 and L2 characterizing lower stages in foreign-language proficiency. Vibrant gestures and other perilingual behaviors may function as supports to deficient verbal articulation. The second thread of reasoning refers to the concepts of cultural scripts (Wierzbicka, 1994, 1999) and the *culture frame switch* (CFS) mechanism elaborated by Benet-Martinez (Boski & Iben Youssef, 2012; Hong et al., 2000; Ramírez-Esparza & García-Sierra, 2014). Communication is a complex interactive system where linguistic and sociocultural elements (e.g., respect, politeness) are mutually integrated and congruent. The mechanism of culture frame switch in conversation behaviors should be expected at more balanced levels of bilingualism. Patrzałek (2020) designed research to test these rival hypotheses. She assumed, though, that international students would present a relatively unbalanced profile of bilingualism, with their perilingual behaviors compensating for L2 deficiencies.

Video-recorded conversations between two actors were her research materials. The actors were Poles and Turks, male students, watching together the final dramatic moments of a football (soccer) match, and then discussing the game. The dyads were (i) monocultural (PL ↔ PL; TR ↔ TR) or (ii) mixed (PL ↔ TR). Accordingly, the interlocutors spoke either their mother tongue (L1: PL or TR) or English (L2) when the dyads were mixed. The design is illustrated in Figure 10.

The video-recorded conversations were watched by research participants who came from the same ethnolinguistic groups: Poles and Turks. Thus, the experiment was a 3-factorial: 2 (Actor: PL | TR) x 2 (Language: L1 |L2) x 2 (Observers: PL | TR). The same person appeared as an actor in both linguistic conditions. The research questions were whether he would behave differently across the two episodes and whether in-group and out-group observers would perceive him as such.

Three situations, marked in Figure 10, need more explanation. The first is when the conversation takes place in L1 between two compatriots (two Poles or two Turks). It is effortless in production and comprehension for both partners and their peer audience. When the interlocutors come from different cultures and they use L2 (English) as the mode of communication, it is a situation of moderate difficulty for all parties involved. Finally, we turn back to two partners speaking their mother tongue but being watched by an audience unfamiliar with that language (e.g., Poles listening to the conversation of two Turks). It reminds us of watching a foreign film without subtitles. On the semantic level, there is a lack of understanding, but viewers may reach some understanding by watching the action and nonverbal cues.

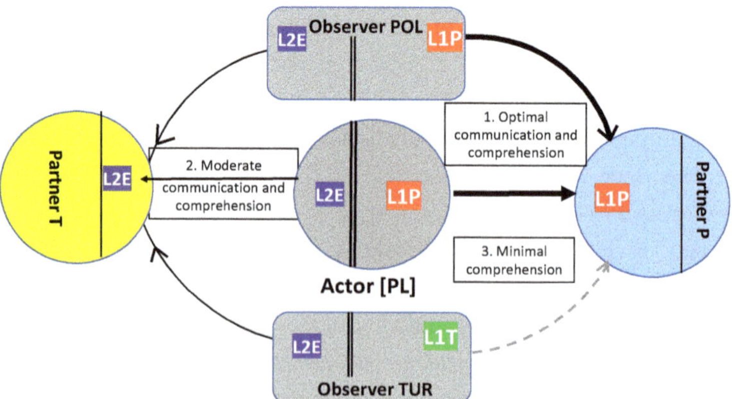

Figure 10 Research design in Patrzałek's (2020) study of perilingual behaviors in bilinguals' L1 and L2 conversations

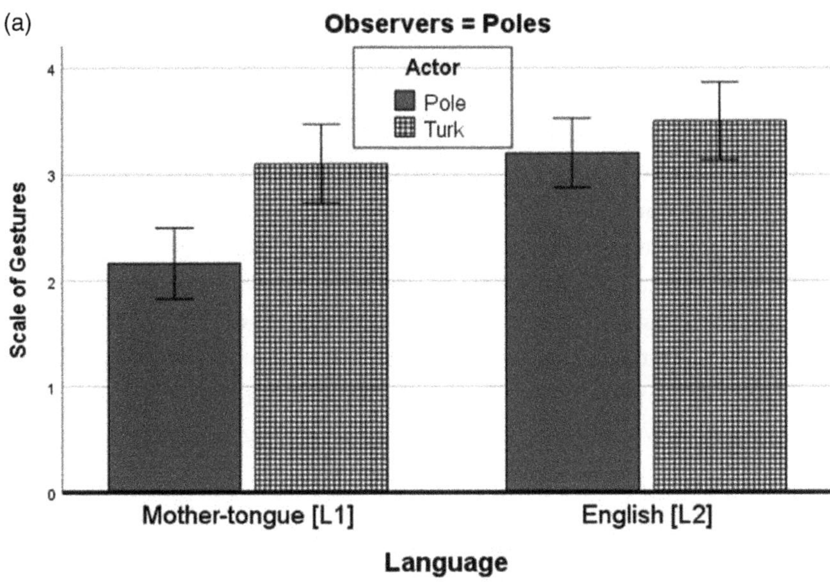

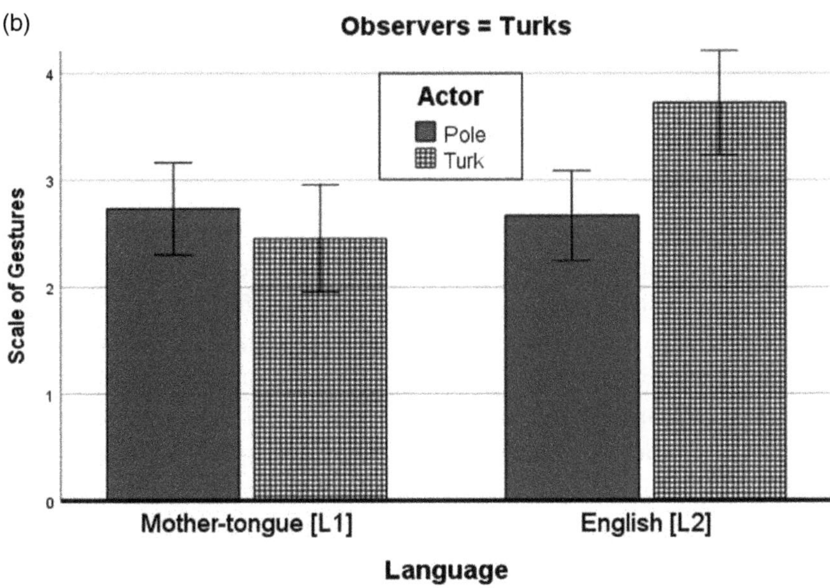

Figure 11 Gestures accompanying conversation in (a) L1 (Polish or Turkish) versus in (b) L2 (English), as perceived by in-group and out-group observers (Patrzałek, 2020)

The actors' perceived gestures and smiles were measured for their intensity and frequency. Figure 11 reveals the results for gestures.

The Turkish actor was perceived as more vibrant than his Polish counterpart; what is theoretically of more importance, observers assessed the intensity of actors' gestures as substantially more pronounced in L2 (English) than when they conversed in their mother tongues (all differences were significant, $p <$ 0.001). In the next step in our analyses, we wanted to check the observer effect when watching actors speaking their mother tongue (L1) versus another tongue (L2). As illustrated in Figure 10, watching actors conversing in L1, which is either familiar or unfamiliar to the observers, makes a large difference. Figure 11 illustrates these findings. A three-way interaction of actor and observer ethnolinguistic categories, and of conversations in the mother tongue versus another tongue as a repeated factor, has proven that noticeable differences of more vibrant gestures in L2 than L1 are perceived only when observers are themselves L1 speakers (Poles for Polish conversations and Turks for Turkish conversations). Watching an L1 speaker whose language is unfamiliar does not create any difference vis-à-vis his L2 conversation.

Unlike gesturing, smiling is a partner-beneficent behavior. Here, the pattern of results was different than before. The Turkish actor was overall perceived as considerably more irradiant than his Polish counterpart. Apart from this main effect, results for his smiling repeated those for gestures: it was more intense when conversing in L2 than in L1. This was contrary to the Polish actor, who was perceived as more reserved to his out-group partner than to the L1 compatriot.

4.3.2 Symbols and Memes

The public space in which people spend their lifetime contains architectural, urban, logistic, and institutional elements that carry relatively universal and instrumental meaning, enabling migrant foreigners to find their way (a store is a store; a bank is a bank). But beyond that surface is a layer of symbolic meaning that fills that space only for those who have been enculturated or acculturated there. For foreigners, it remains empty. The temporal aspect of that space is a cultural calendar, which lends certain days meaning and importance while remaining unfamiliar to visitors. Finally, public heroes, celebrities, teams, and artists enter that space and attract attention, but, again, not for out-group members. To put it bluntly, a migrant can live in the host country meeting his/ her economic goals of saving and remitting funds (see Section 2) without participating in this noosphere.

Waning of Symbolic Knowledge and Cathexis with Time and Generations

Symbols have been part of this model of acculturation since its inception forty years ago in my initial investigations on Polish immigrants in America. For technical reasons, they were presented via a verbal channel (not as pictures,

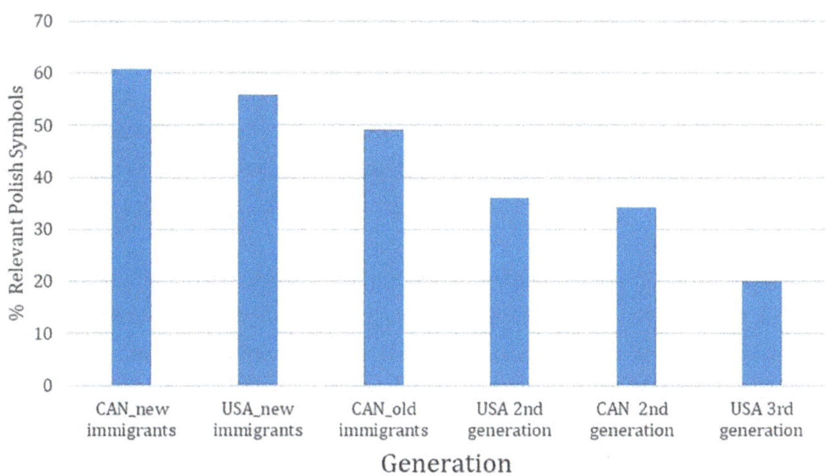

Figure 12 The decline of known and cathected symbols in three generations
(1–2–3) of Polish immigrants to Canada and the United States
(*young* and *old* refer to the cohorts: post–World War II and 1980s immigrants,
respectively)

which is now the standard). Two questions were asked about each item: (i) Do you know what it is? (ii) Do you care for it? Figure 12 presents percentages of Polish symbols cared for (or cathected) in three generations of Polish-Americans and Polish-Canadians.

It is clearly illustrated that as we move from the most recent first-generation immigrants to the third generation, there is a linear decline in the size of personally important symbols. Symbolic vitality requires continuous refreshing reappearances; otherwise, it fades away. Lewandowska (2008) obtained similar results in her study on second-generation immigrants in the United Kingdom.

Home Country Symbols, Affect, and Subjective Well-Being

Over the years, we have collected enough evidence to assert that symbolic identity with the culture of origin enhances mood and SWB among immigrants. In the Polish-American studies just mentioned, the speed of response (RTs) to personally relevant home country symbols was the top predictor of the level of happiness on Cantril's Ladder (Boski, 1994). In a study with Vietnamese immigrants (Boski, 2022, ch. 13), photos of the *Quê Hương* (Toward the Homeland) restaurant in Warsaw and of the World War II Warsaw Uprising monument were very strong positive and negative predictors of SWLS, respectively (both explained 30% of its variance). Finally, Biernacka (2010; Boski, 2022) measured mood and life satisfaction among Brazilian expatriates/sojourners in Poland, with

Poles serving as a control group. Participants in the experimental condition were shown a video of the previous year's Carnival in Rio (a samba street procession); no such display occurred in the control condition. The Carnival video boosted participants' temporal positive mood (PANAS), but the effect was more pronounced among Brazilians than among Poles. Also, following exposure to that video (and not in the control condition), Brazilians declared higher life satisfaction than Poles.

A large study on symbolic identity among Mauritians was conducted by Dabee (2021), a national of this multicultural island state in the Indian Ocean. Mauritius has no Indigenous population, and its complicated ethnolinguistic structure is a legacy of the colonial period under the rule of France and the United Kingdom. Ethnolinguistic pluralism is the reality of Mauritian society and multiculturalism is its goal. Dabee's research problem was to investigate the linguistic and symbolic aspects of Mauritian identity and their impact on well-being.

Based on official ethnic categories (sanctioned by the constitution) and by the languages participants used in their daily lives, three clusters were extracted. Three languages – Kreol, French, and English – were in common use, indistinguishable between the clusters. Indo-Mauritians speaking all three formed cluster 1 (n = 114), while other descendants from the Indian peninsula, who spoke additionally some of the ancestral languages (Hindi, Bhojpuri) were included in cluster 2 (n = 177). Finally, minorities (Creole, Muslims, Sino-Mauritians) made up cluster 3 (n = 154), irrespective of whether they spoke any other language in addition to the three principal ones.

Although the three languages were in common use, they were domain specific. Dabee asked her participants in which language would they contact each of the twenty-two stimulus persons (marked on photos) when entering a conversation with them. Those target individuals were photographed in workplace situations (e.g., a street seller, bus conductor, teacher, or physician). Although lower-status individuals would be almost exclusively contacted in Kreol, the language of conversation with higher-status interlocutors would be predominantly French (English was the lowest).

Another set of fifty pictorial symbols was selected in consultation with local experts. These symbols covered items in such categories as geography, architecture, food, and dress. Some of them were nationally unifying while other symbolic pictures reflected narrower ethnic identities. The author found positive correlations between symbolic national identity and the frequency of using Kreol and a symmetric but negative correlation with the readiness to address compatriots in English (which is an official language at the governmental level in Mauritius).

As in other studies reported in this section, symbolic identity was hypothesized as a predictor of SWB. Unlike in classical investigations, where SWB is an individual-level variable, we also used a scale of family well-being. This inventory mimics Diener's well-known scale and was proposed by Kryś and colleagues (2019a, 2019b). Familial SWLS seems very appropriate in a cultural context where family collectivism is the prime dimension. Mauritius is such a culture. We regressed both measures of SWB on symbolic identity scores, receiving meaningful results only for the family-oriented scale. For the whole sample, which included the three ethnolinguistic groups mentioned earlier, the size of their ethnic symbols was a negative predictor of familial SWLS. However, when the three ethnolinguistic groups were split for separate analyses, the size of nationally unifying symbols among the minority category of Créols and Muslims who occupy the lowest social status in the country positively predicted familial SWLS.

Linguistic and symbolic elements of cultural identity go closely together, reinforcing each other. We have learned from Dabee's research on Mauritius that the more often participants used Kreol in their daily conversations, the larger the size of symbols they considered as all-national (compared to ethnic only). Conversely, the use of English was negatively related to national symbolic identity. Similarly, in a two-wave study conducted in Ukraine just prior to and half a year after Russia launched its military attack, we found that symbols of national identity mattered significantly more for Ukrainian-speaking citizens than for Russian-speaking citizens of that country (Boski et al., 2024).[22]

Altogether, our findings have shown that a broader symbolic identity is beneficial for minorities to overcome their families' marginalized status and to feel more a part of a larger community; fencing off has the opposite, deteriorating effects on family life satisfaction. To conclude, symbolic cultural identity has positive effects on life satisfaction in all studies reported in this section.[23] They also strengthen broader communal identities in conjunction with the usage of the national language. These effects may be momentary because the nostalgic reactivation of emotions initially accompanying symbols is short-lived. People may seek the reoccurrence of such circumstances, which provide them with positive hedonic value, though.

Memes: A Convolution of Pictorial Symbols and Verbal Content

Memes form an interesting cultural phenomenon that has appeared recently in popular culture. Dawkins (1976) introduced the term to denote a unit of cultural replication and transmission by social imitation. In their current popular use,

---

[22] The law making the Ukrainian language official and compulsory in education and in all domains of public life was passed during President Poroshenko's term in office. Still, in practical terms, millions of citizens have used Russian as a first language, particularly in the eastern regions of the country.

[23] A word of caution is needed here. Symbolic images of tragic events that lead to refugee exodus and reactivate people's trauma are not included here. They do not count as representative of the culture in question, though.

memes are short messages commenting on current events in a satirical way, similar to traditional caricatures, which are spread on the Internet. Memes combine words and pictures. Words are usually used as puns, which require advanced linguistic competence. Pictures are often transformed into morphs, presenting two characters at once (e.g., a historical figure and its current alter ego).

Because of their concise form and layers of semantic depth, memes are excellent means for studying first-culture as well as second-culture understanding. Figure 13 illustrates two memes, one American and one Polish, used in Jasińska's (2023) study on Polish-American mixed couples.

The American meme should be easily identifiable and understood by an English-language user and perhaps worldwide, but it requires some knowledge of US history as well. It is a mockery of a former US president whose plan to counteract illegal immigration was to build a wall at the border with Mexico. A Native American Indian chief responds regretfully to this rhetoric: "Why didn't we think of that?" – that is, to banish White colonizers some 200 years earlier when they started coming to America.

The Polish meme will most likely be answered correctly only by Poles and perhaps by the second generation of immigrants attending Polish schools. Seen

Figure 13 (a) American and **(b)** Polish memes used by Jasińska (2023)

in the picture is Adam Mickiewicz, a nineteenth-century national bard. The romantic poetic style of his oeuvres is mimicked in the meme's verbal output, which reflects today's commercial market reality. The sarcastic transformation refers to the recent ban on commercial business activities in Poland on Sundays: "And I saw a nation hanging around aimlessly – Lidl being closed and so was Biedronka."[24] Here, the historic literary material is intertwined with contemporary consumerism: people are confused; they feel lost, not knowing what to do when the shopping malls are closed.

A series of open-ended questions is attached to each meme for participants to answer. First, they are asked about iconic character identification and the surface sense of the verbal content, which can be called cultural perception. Next, we probe for the events that are referred to and the hidden meaning of words (a pun) in association with the pictorial layer of the meme. Finally, we pose a question about the main message the meme conveys. Based on a Goddess Kali vs. Virgin Mary study (Boski, 2018), an answer coding system has been proposed in the form of a five-point scale measuring the level of meme comprehension:

0 = no central figure(s) identification or wrong identification. No proper understanding of the surface verbal message.

1–1.5 = identification of main characters (e.g., their functions; it is President Trump). Understanding of the surface verbal message.

2 = identification of the broader context surrounding the central figure's activity or state (e.g., to prevent illegal immigration, President Trump started building a wall at the US–Mexico border; the closing of Lidl/Biedronka supermarkets on Sundays deprived Poles of their preferred entertainment).

3 = cultural interpretation of the message depicted by the meme (e.g., protection of country borders in two periods, one historical and the other contemporary, to highlight that Indigenous people could have banned Whites from America; a humorous juxtaposition of nineteenth-century romantic patriotic poetry and today's trivial shopping).

4 = an expert icon interpretation: the breadth (context) and depth (historical, moral) of the story (e.g., those planning to build a protecting wall now should remember their ancestors were intruders who could have been fenced off by Indigenous people; mindless consumerism takes away people's deeper sense of life).

For the past couple of years, our students have been completing meme projects as group tasks in a course on acculturation psychology. With several hundred

---

[24] Lidl and Biedronka are two popular commercial chains of grocery stores in Poland.

reports, we may conclude that the surface verbal layer is much better understood by Slavic students due to linguistic proximity, while no such differences have been noticed in valid identification of pictorial symbolic representation of chief figures in Polish public life. An in-depth, expert-level cultural interpretation was generally missing.

Jasińska (2023) used memes more systematically in her work on Polish-American couples. Her research problem was the relationship between marital satisfaction and cultural identity structures. Polish spouses answered American memes while their American partners addressed Polish memes. Her results revealed huge differences in cultural competence between the partners of these couples. Polish spouses (mostly women) were vastly superior to their American partners in the level of C2 meme interpretation (Cohen $d = 1.23$). Although this difference in cultural competence scores has not been related to marital satisfaction (within or between the couples), it shows an interesting phenomenon of cultural imbalance: American culture shows a clear dominance. Not only do mixed marriages communicate in English and not in Polish, but also at the symbolic level, Polish spouses know much more about their partners' culture than the reverse.

Memes present new cultural phenomena all over the world and, except for this preliminary report, I have not found any enculturation or acculturation study exploiting them. More can be expected to come from our lab.

4.3.3 Cultural Values and Identities: Research Strategies

Unlike language and symbols that belong to either C1 or C2 and rarely to both cultural systems jointly, such distinctiveness does not characterize *values and practices*. While it is an easy task to identify a person who wears a flag pinned to the lapel of his/her jacket, it is not equally evident if that person expresses English or Polish values or behaves according to them. Three reasons can be advanced to account for this difference: (i) the discrete nature of languages and symbols versus the continuous nature of values; (ii) more ingroup variance (less consensus) in the value-normative domain than in language and symbols; and (iii) it is harder to assess whether a person behaved properly regarding his/her cultural norms. Based on these differences, it takes three steps of a relational procedure to establish one's cultural, axionormative identity. This process will now be described as it has evolved over a thirty-year research period.

Cultural values and identities: A prototype-based approach. This method was initially employed during the 1980s and 1990s in a research program on Polish immigrants in Canada and the United States. Designed for that work, the Cultural

Values and Scripts Inventory (CVSI) consisted of sixty-six items covering various domains of societal life (see Boski, 1991, for more details).[25] Participants attempted self-reports and those of Polish and American prototypes. Prototypes were sketchy portrayals of several individuals depicted by their demographics, vocation, type of work, and political orientation (e.g., first/family name, a forty-year-old technician at the Gdańsk shipyard, married with two children, actively involved in the SOLIDARNOŚĆ trade union, opposed to the ruling communist party). From a list of about ten prototypes belonging to their home and host country, participants would choose characters they considered the *typical, most positive*, or *most negative* personification of each culture. The responses were forced into a Q-sort normal distribution format. Cultural identity was measured as a correlation coefficient between self-report and a prototype.

Several results from the reported studies (Boski, 1988b, 1991, 1992) deserve attention:

(i) Set between monocultural Poles and Americans, Polish immigrants manifested a bicultural identity, where the Polish component was generally stronger than the American.

(ii) Positive cultural identity was asymmetrically stronger than negative identity. However, negative prototypes and identities were more similar cross-culturally than their positive expressions, which differed in intensity of humane orientation, stronger on the Polish side.

(iii) Normative acculturation toward biculturalism was more easily accomplished with women than with men.

(iv) Across time and generations, the process toward normative bicultural balance was happening through the shrinking distance between the prototypes and not by changes occurring in the self.

The last result is theoretically the most interesting because it modifies our understanding of psychological change; from the angle of actor-participants, this occurred through the shortening of cultural distance between the prototypes, while the self remained intact.

---

[25] The items were derived from pilot interviews with immigrants, personal observations, and consultations with experts. For example: *The law is the law; it is observed strictly and without any exceptions. Buying a house, then renting or selling it at a profit, then buying a better one is a way to improve one's socioeconomic status* (American). *Spend long hours discussing and debating hot political issues; readily offer people selfless compassion and a helpful hand* (Polish). Popular in the field, Schwartz's personality and values questionnaire (PVQ) inventory (Schwartz et al., 2012), could not be used for our purposes. There, participants are required to compare themselves to an imaginary but culturally nonspecific person who endorses a given value. With Schwartz's methodology, there is no provision for culture-level assessment independent from personal values assessment.

                    Psychology and Culture

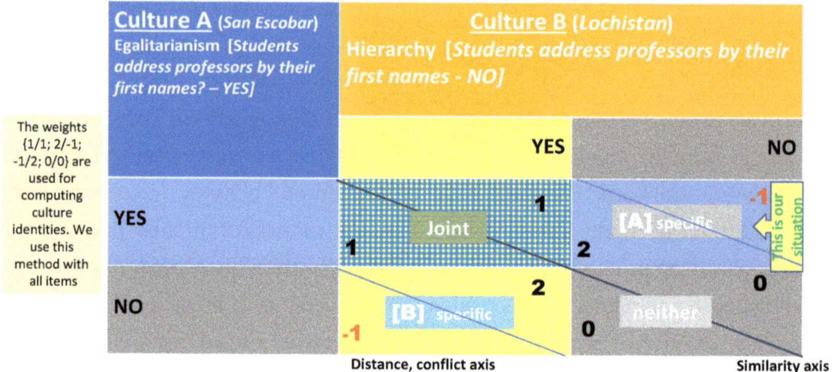

Figure 14 Culture descriptive task in the measurement of bicultural normative identity

Cultural descriptors, personal preferences, and their products as identity indices.

Over time, the operationalization of normative acculturation has been modified, including a three-step measurement procedure.

Culture descriptors (CDs). Rather than using personalized prototypes, we have decided to measure culture A and B values (practices, scripts) simultaneously by their cross-section. Figure 14 presents a double-dichotomized matrix of this sorting task.

Thus research participants are asked to compare the two cultures by distributing the set of sixty-six CVSI items into four cells spread along two axes: (i) the *similarity axis* has two instances, occurring when a given item is assigned to both cultures with equal weights (1/1) or to neither of them (0/0); (ii) the two instances along *difference axes* take place when its presence in one culture coincides with the absence in the other. When an item is found typical for C1 culture but not for C2, the weights assume (2/−1) magnitudes; an opposite pair of weights (−1/2) is assigned to the reverse situation (C1 = No and C2 = Yes). These weights are to some extent arbitrary but backed by the logic of intercultural comparison. The four weights for each item show a descending order {2, 1, 0, −1} in each culture: from highest (2) for unique presence, through non-specificity (1 or 0), to an absence (−1) relative to the other culture.[26]

This rather abstract format of the sorting task is exemplified by an item covering the communication script of students addressing their university instructors. Depending on power distance (or hierarchy), in some countries, the norm is to

---

[26] In some studies, the cross-sectional analysis of two cultures is done in a 3 x 3 matrix where the third answer – "I don't know"/"hard to say" – supplements the yes/no dichotomy.

use academic titles: Madame Professor X, Sir Doctor Y, and so forth. Elsewhere, in egalitarian cultures, it is customary to call instructors by their first names. I use the names of two fictitious countries, Lochistan and San Escobar, to further explain the general rule. If an international exchange student arrives from egalitarian San Escobar to hierarchical Lochistan, then the cultural discrepancy between them will soon be detected in classroom behaviors reflecting the right-hand upper cell of Figure 14 (San Escobar Yes = 2; Lochistan No = −1, for the use of first names).

Personal preferences. The second step of the procedure consists of measuring individual value preferences on the same set of items that served to compare both cultures (except the items being framed in the singular I, instead of impersonal culture descriptors). The Likert-type responses range from strongly disagree = −2, through neutral = 0, to +2 = strongly agree, for each item.

Normative bicultural identity. Neither culture descriptions nor individual preferences alone can serve as indices of cultural identity. For this to happen, the two components should be combined by a multiplication function; this procedure is illustrated in Figure 15.

To continue the example introduced in Figure 14, for a San Escobarian student whose culture is egalitarian concerning interpersonal communication [+2], and that he/she likes personally [+2], the San Escobarian identity is 2 x 2 = 4. In Lochistan, where that person is a sojourner and where an opposite script is practiced, his/her score would be −1 x 2 = −2. Altogether, the components of home culture identity (CI) can be:

(i) positive, when the unique or joint presence of CD is met with acceptance of corresponding personal values (PVs) (e.g., CD_{+2} x PV_{+2} = CI_{+4}) or when a CD's miss co-occurs with its rejection at the personal level (e.g., CD_{-1} x PV_{-2} = CI_{+2}, *It is not ours and I do not like it*);

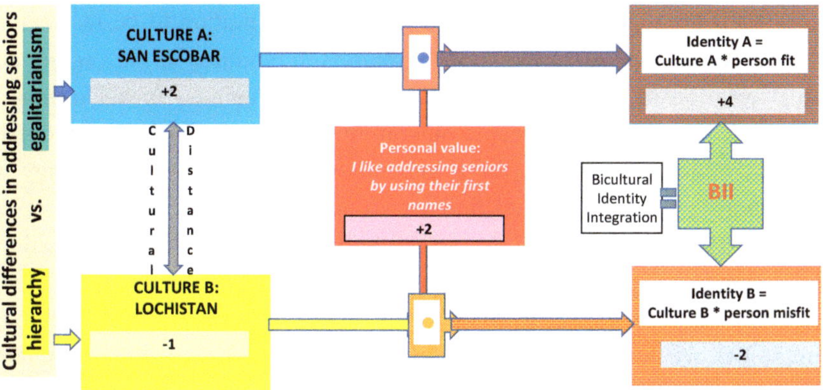

Figure 15 Conceptual scheme of bicultural normative identity as a product of culture descriptions and individual preferences

(ii) zero, when either the CD or the PV has been rated at this level;

(iii) negative, when the CD's presence is not personally appreciated (e.g., CD_{+2} x PV_{-2} = CI_{-4}, or when its miss co-occurs with personal preference (e.g., CD_{-1} x PV_{+2} = CI_{-2}, *I wish it were like this with us too*).

The total identity score for each culture is a sum of all weighted items across the four options.[27]

Besides total cultural identity, which aggregates all indices just described, partial measures may be of interest too. *Integrated identity* is this fraction that covers the joint space of two cultures. Partial C1 or C2 identities are the sums of weighted PVs in the space covered uniquely by each of them separately from the other [(2|−1) and (−1|2)].

Poland before access to the European Union: An early example of the new measures. The first large study where this new methodological approach was applied came from a nationally representative sample of adult Poles (1,100 participants over eightten years of age) investigating their values at the time of accession to the European Union (EU) (Boski, 2005, 2022). It was not acculturation research in its usual sense; joining a regional organization of nation-states did not entail leaving one's own country or entering into closer contact with any specific nation-state culture. In a technical sense, measuring cultural identity structure followed the steps described earlier in this section. The value items were simultaneously classified into four descriptive ($_Y PL_N$ x $_Y EU_N$) and four personal-evaluative categories: (i) *import* to us, (ii) maintain/ *export*, (iii) ambivalent, and (iv) reject. The domain of common values on both sides was the smallest. The three (out of sixteen) most pronounced combined subcategories of cultural identity were: (i) European virtues of social efficiency and liberalism to be imported as deficient in Poland (17.1%, e.g., *serious approach to tasks at work, being on time, tolerance and open-ness*); (ii) heritage values of Polish humanist orientation to be maintained (11.83%, e.g., *caring for friendships; selfless helpfulness to the needy*); and (iii) rejection of Polish vices (9.90%; e.g., *recklessness in performance; obstinate intransigence*). People most in favor of EU membership endorsed liberal values; they opted for a general overhaul of Polish axiology by rejecting its heritage (virtues and vices) and the importation of European virtues. Those in favor of keeping the humanist legacy of national culture alive remained neutral to the integration with European structures.

From today's perspective of almost two decades of Poland's membership in the EU, we may say that the conflicts that have emerged at the state level

---

[27] The formula for that index reads: CI $= \sum_{(i\,=\,1\ \text{to n})} (CD_i x PV_i)$ where CI = cultural identity; $i_{(1\ \text{to n})}$ item number from 1 to n; CD_i = culture descriptor *i*; PV_i = Personal value *i*.

over the past years were predictable at the birth of the accession process. The findings of twenty years ago that led to this conclusion were: (i) the axis of cultural differences dominated over commonality; (ii) for people most in favor of EU integration, the process of transition was regarded as abandoning national cultural identity, rather than attempting balance between the two entities; (iii) humanism, which has been continuously the leading axiological orientation in the national culture (Boski, 2022; Boski & Darpatova-Hruzewicz, 2023), has not been harnessed into integration.

Recent Acculturation Studies Using the Three-Stage Assessment of Bicultural Identity

Polish-French Acculturation (Kmiotek, 2020, Study #1). While the measurement of cultural identity in the just-reported project was designed at the macro level, we return to individual-level acculturation in the next studies. Kmiotek's (2020, Study #1) work is the first where virtual (remote) acculturation was systematically investigated, as proposed in the general model at the opening of this section. In the context of French-Polish intercultural contacts, he compared university students (in Warsaw and Wrocław) of French language and culture with second-generation immigrant adolescents attending francophone and international high schools in Lyon (France) and in Brussels (Belgium); a group of first-generation economic migrants was also included.

Aggregate identity indices were computed for both cultures according to the formulae (sum of products), and their scores are presented in Figure 16a.

These results resemble those of liberally oriented Euro-enthusiasts from the EU pre-accession study. Here too Polish identity at home is much lower than French (idealized) identity. The opposite profile with dominant Polish identity was found, however, among immigrants residing in France or Belgium. It should be noted, though, that of all partial identities contributing to the aggregate scores for each culture, the joint component (Polish and French) is by far the most pronounced, as can be seen in Figure 16b, and this tendency is stronger with the immigrant groups. The largest differences between the five categories of participants are found in the Polish partial identity component, shrunk in university student groups ($p < 0.001$).

The results on cultural identities conform to the adage that the grass is always greener on the other side and can be interpreted along the lines of studies on nostalgia (Wildschut et al., 2006) or an idealistic orientation (Weinreich & Saunderson, 2005).

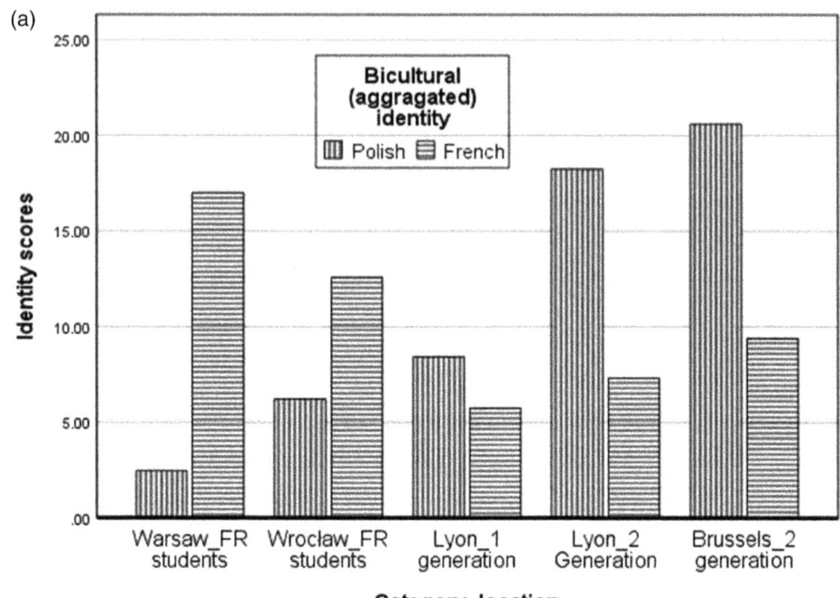

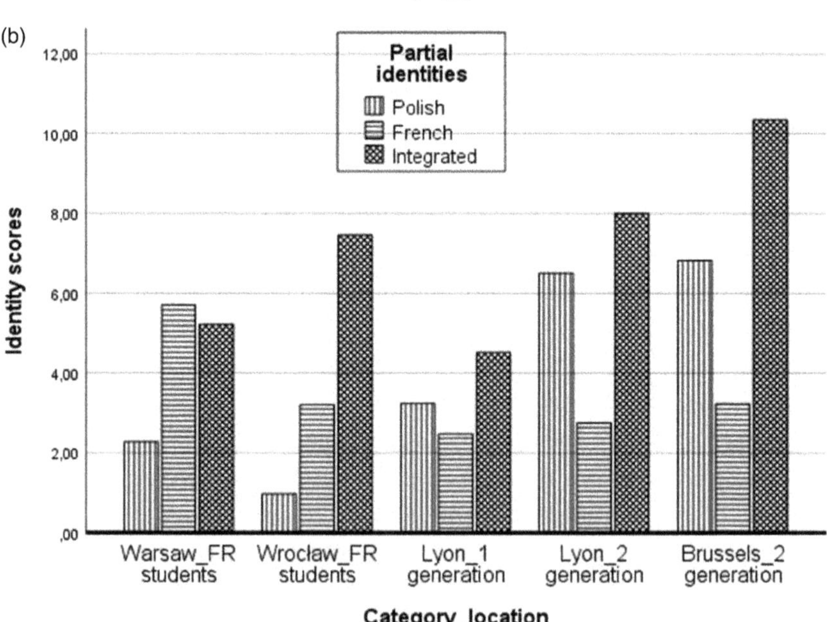

Figure 16 Polish–French bicultural identities (a) global aggregated; (b) partial indices (Kmiotek, 2020, Study #1)

Immigrants from South Asia to Northwestern Europe (Tariq, 2023; Sharmin, 2021**).** Compared to Poland and France, the cultural distance between southern Asia and the countries of northwestern Europe is objectively much

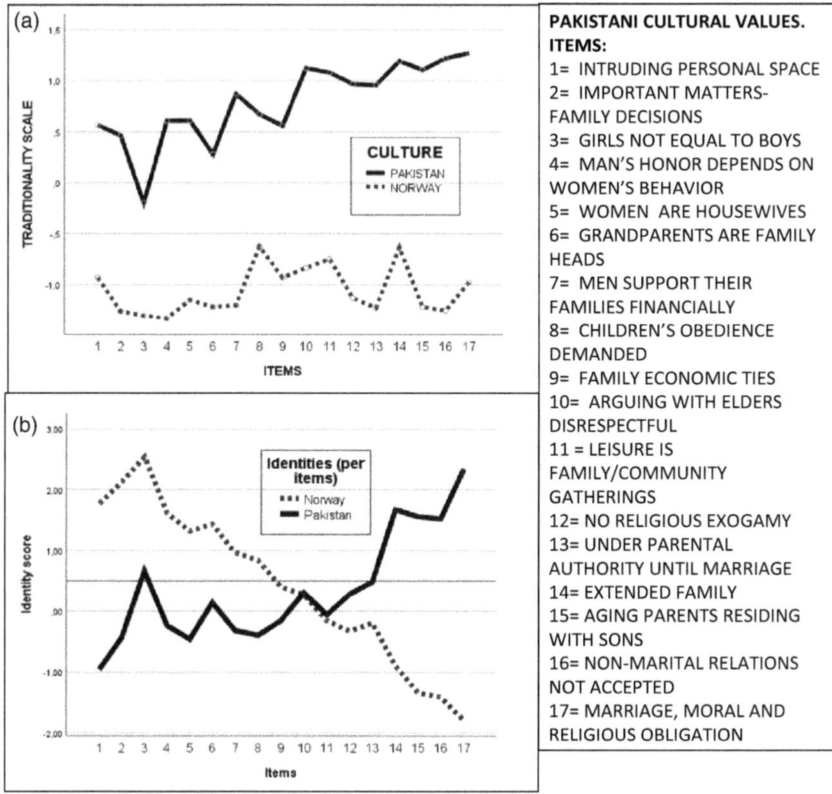

Figure 17 Bicultural identity of Pakistani immigrants in Norway: (a) cultural descriptors of the two countries; (b) identity score per item and item clusters (Tariq, 2023)

larger. Pakistan and Bangladesh are two officially Muslim republics. They practice extended family systems and arranged marriages; the role of women in hierarchical patriarchy is subordinate to that of men. Also, when compared to northwestern Europe, a wide contrast between the interdependent and independent self has been reported (Vignoles et al., 2016).

Tariq (2023) studied two generations of Pakistani immigrants in Norway. A set of seventeen cultural descriptors was used to compare these two cultures. Cultural experts from both sides were consulted on item construction and selection. Rather than presenting the mean scores of all items or their factorial scales, the differences are illustrated with singular measures in Figure 17a.

Each item is worded in its traditional version, and for each of them, Norway is well below Pakistan (all $p_s < 0.001$). These two cultures present mirror images of one another. Acculturation between such opposites presents a big challenge. How it worked with the sample of Pakistani immigrants can be seen in Figure 17b.

Due to changes in some personal values (especially in the second born-in-Norway generation), we can observe a partial identity shift. It occurs in the domain called equality and individuation, being particularly noticeable for gender and age egalitarianism. However, the second factorial domain – that is, the fundamental values of tight family and marriage norms – has been maintained as the core of Pakistani identity. These two tendencies have been strongly contrasted between generations. Participants born in the host country scored higher on Norwegian equality and individuation; those who migrated from Pakistan insisted more on the maintenance of family traditions ($p_s < 0.001$). Finally, only the second identity component, that of family traditions, mattered for life satisfaction (measured with the SWLS). Immigrants who switched to Norwegian, nuclear, and secular types of family life suffered a loss in life satisfaction ($r[112] = -0.239$, $p < 05$) and the loss was greater for the second generation ($r[65] = -0.341$, $p < 0.01$). Calling this Pakistani-Norwegian bicultural identity "integration" would lack precision. What we observe instead is a partial change and partial maintenance, which are most likely adaptive to life in two very different cultures.

Sharmin's (2021) study on Bangladeshi immigrants in the United Kingdom was designed in a similar way to that by Tariq, including a considerable overlap of the two values/practices questionnaires.[28] The items appear next to Figure 18.

Here we have again a large axio-normative distance between two cultures. All twenty-eight CDs depicted in Figure 18a differ significantly between Bangladesh and the United Kingdom (in most cases, well below $p < 0.001$). Particularly interesting is the crossing point at item 19: *Direct communication is preferred even if it disrupts the harmony with others*, where the linear order of the means for both countries has changed: British values surpass the Bangladeshi. Thus, on the left of this crossover, we have the predominantly Bangladeshi values of family collectivism and interdependence, while on the right-hand side, we have the British value of an independent self.[29]

When it comes to bicultural identities (Figure 18b), their profiles do not reflect the profiles of CDs in a simple, symmetrical way. Even within the set of traditional family collectivism and self-interdependence values, Bangladeshi immigrants in the United Kingdom experience an identity shift. They

---

[28] Indeed, Sharmin's study is of an earlier date. Also, besides immigrants, her sample included Bangladeshi and British participants, residents in their countries, the overall size of her sample was $n = 114$.

[29] The picture portrayed in Figure 18a could be more one-sided, like in Figure 17a, with Tariq's data if British values were transformed to their negatives and became consistent with the Bangladeshi worldview. The reason for the format in which they are presented is the scoring system applied in Sharmin's study, consistent with that illustrated in Figure 14.

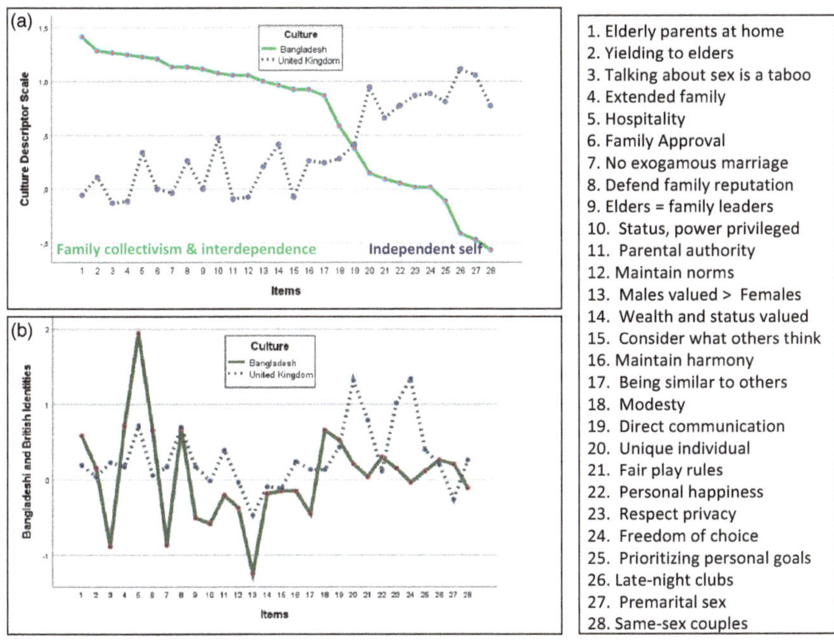

Figure 18 Bicultural identity of Bangladeshi immigrants in the United Kingdom (Sharmin, 2021) (a) Bangladeshi versus British values; (b) Bangladeshi and British identities

particularly reject the traditional values of female subordinate roles and the ban on exogamous marriages.

Subjective well-being was measured in Sharmin's study with the popular Diener SWLS scale and also with its family well-being version (e.g., *In most ways, the life of my family is close to ideal. My family is satisfied with its life* [Kryś et al., 2019b]). We compared the effectiveness of PVs and identity indicators as predictors of these two outcome variables. The results of these regression analyses are important for testing the whole three-step model of axio-normative identity. We predicted that identity measures would be better predictors than PVs alone, particularly in the case of family well-being. Multiple regression analyses were performed on singular items rather than compound measures, following the pattern of presentation in Figure 18. Results confirmed these expectations. While PVs predicted familial and individual SWLS scores by singular items and at a very low level ($R^2_{adj.} = 0.107$; and $R^2_{adj.} = 0.126$, respectively), the accuracy of predictions by cultural identity measures was much higher. Four Bangladeshi identity items predicted familial SWPS at $R^2_{adj.} = 0.325$, and for five British identity items, this coefficient was even higher, $R^2_{adj.} = 0.397$. Also, similarly to Dabee's work in Mauritius, it was family (and not personal) life satisfaction that was related to cultural identity indices.

4.3.4 Bicultural Identity Integration (BII)

With these research examples, I concentrated on various identity measures that the theoretical framework can generate. The two cultures filling the acculturating person's living space may remain in mutually complex conditions. They are seen in Figure 14 along diagonals of integration and conflict, and in Figure 15 where the construct of BII = Bicultural Identity Integration was introduced. Bicultural identity integration is the theory associated predominantly with the works of Veronica Benet-Martinez and her colleagues (Benet-Martinez et al., 2002; Benet-Martinez, Lee & Leu, 2006; Benet-Martinez & Haritatos, 2005; Chen, Benet-Martinez & Bond, 2008). According to that author, bicultural identity is a complex meta-structure that may assume different forms and dimensions. The first of them was proposed as a bipolar scale**: Harmony** (*I find it easy to harmonize A and B cultures*) versus **Conflict** (*I feel caught between cultures A and B*). The other dimension is a bipolar scale of **Blendedness** (*I feel A and B at the same time*) versus **Compartmentalization** (*I keep A and B cultures separate*).

I call BII a meta-construct because it is overlaid on primary identity measures obtained separately for each culture. In the theoretical model presented in this Element, identity integration results from the composition of CDs: (i) high when the two are perceived as similar, and (ii) low when their differences prevail. Also, the sum of negative products of (culture descriptors x individual preferences) contributes to low BII. In Sharmin's study, one significant correlation was found between the index of integration operationalized as the sum of products for values shared in both cultures and the BII scale of blendedness – compartmentalization ($r_{53} = -.32, p < .05$). This indicates that immigrants with high scores in a shared home and host culture identity manifested their tendency to experience and express their Bangladeshi and Britishness separately rather than jointly.

The BII compartmentalization was also very effectively predicted ($R^2_{adj.} = 0.475$) by five identity items. Bangladeshi immigrants who kept and practiced their two cultures separately were characterized by (i) accepting Bangladeshi lack of consent for premarital sex, and (ii) Bangladeshis' penchant for etiquette; (iii) they did not agree with the British philosophy of personal happiness separate from family well-being; (iv) they appreciated British hospitality (even if much lower than Bangladeshi hospitality); and (v) they did not agree with the British cultural concept of direct communication.

Conclusion regarding the studies by Kmiotek, Tariq, and Sharmin. A couple of results from the last three studies deserve attention. First, Kmiotek's work brought evidence for prevalence of remote axio-normative identity. There was a noticeably stronger attachment to the values of heritage culture among the second-generation Polish immigrant youth, and idealized French values among their student counterparts residing in Poland. The mechanism of nostalgia, as postulated by Sedikides and his colleagues (2009) seems to explain these phenomena. At the same time, the bicultural element of each aggregate identity index by far exceeds any of its monocultural components.

This strong and convincing finding brings us closer to the construct of integration, central to Berry's model and critically discussed earlier in this Element. Given these similarities, the question to be addressed is as follows: are Berry's integration and the present author's joint component of bicultural identity the same thing? In answering this question, one should be reminded that Berry's integration is a construct of preferences, measured as attitudes (e.g., *I feel that [ethnic group] should maintain our cultural traditions but also adopt those of [national]*). In my approach, it all starts with the cross-section of CDs, which are framed in a neutral, descriptive mode. Preferences are introduced in the next step when they are bonded with descriptors as PVs, forming joint as well as specific cultural identities with C1 and C2. Neither of the latter is equivalent to preferences for separation or assimilation, but each represents participants' experience within a bicultural space.

Tariq's and Sharmin's studies demonstrate two acculturation settings where home and host cultures are much more distant than Poland and France, where the size of joint descriptors was the largest. Indeed, immigrants from Pakistan and Bangladesh found the traditionality of their cultures of origin significantly higher in general and on each item, than in the Norwegian and British cultures, respectively. The item-by-item analyses were used to demonstrate these effects. A bicultural identity shift was observed in the Pakistani–Norwegian context, such that immigrants changed their values in the direction of egalitarianism in public life, but retained loyalty to extended family collectivism and norms of arranged marriages.

In the Bangladeshi–British context, bicultural identity demonstrated selectivity on both sides of the spectrum and a compartmentalized profile. Bangladeshi immigrants in the United Kingdom separated the two components of their identity. In addition, home culture identity was weaker among Bangladeshi immigrants, than host culture identity. This coincided with similar results in monocultural groups where British paticipants largely outscored their counterparts in Bangladesh. Finally, our theoretical model was successfully validated by highly accurate predictions of (family) life satisfaction by compound identity (products) items, compared to the same set of personal values.

4.3.5 Mutual Triangulation in a Tripartite Model

The active role of language in the cognitive representation of reality. So far, all three pillars of acculturation have been discussed separately even though their interconnections were theoretically assumed and empirically expected. We take it from Wittgenstein (2009/1953) that language is not just an "objective" reflection of reality, but being a part of the culture, it co-constructs our representations of the world. This philosophical approach belongs to the same class as the Sapir–Whorf hypothesis, which postulates cultural relativism in cognition. Among contemporary scholars asserting the active role of language in cognition, Anna Wierzbicka (1994, 1999, 2010) and Deborah Roberson (2012; Roberson, Davidoff & Shapiro, 2002; Roberson, Davies & Davidoff, 2000) are the leading authors.

Roberson is known predominantly for her research on categorical perception of color. Because languages cut the visible color spectrum with an uneven number of basic color words (a range from two to twelve), perceptual categories and their boundaries differ between most European languages (including English with its eleven basic terms) and Berinmo (in Papua New Guinea) or Himba (Namibia), which operate with only five color words.

Based on that discrepancy between physical reality and linguistic categories, Roberson and her colleagues found that English and Himba or Berinmo participants differed in their judgments about the similarity of color tiles (chips) being objectively at equal distances on the Munsell color system. Two tiles that fell in the same linguistic color category in one language would be perceived as belonging to different categories in the other language. (Similar effects were found on color recognition tasks.) I refer to these findings because they demonstrate an active role of language in reality construction at a fundamental level of visual perception. Now we can move to values, which represent a more advanced level of human psychology, and where the connection between language and axiology is more persuasive.

Anna Wierzbicka, who wrote profusely on emotional differences between languages, has been equally eloquent at the level of philosophical abstractions. In her treatise *Experience, Evidence, & Sense* (Wierzbicka, 2010), she analyzed the three English concepts of that book title as the key concepts of British culture. Their foundations lie in British eighteenth-century empiricist philosophy (e.g., John Locke, David Hume), but the origins are traced earlier, found also in Shakespeare's dramas. Although they sound quite international, these words can hardly be translated into other languages:

> The concept of *experience* plays a vital role in English speakers' ways of thinking and provides the prism through which they interpret the world. While its range of use is broad [. . .] several of these senses have a common theme that reflects a characteristically Anglo perspective on the world and human life. This is why the word *experience* is often untranslatable (without distortion) in other languages, even European languages. (Wierzbicka, 2010, p. 31)

In Polish, the term *experience* conveys three meanings covered by three different words: (i) a method of empirical investigation (*experiment*); (ii) a sensation (e.g., visual, auditory), translatable as *doświadczenie*; and (iii) an affective process after *going through* something (usually harsh), which is *przeżycie*.[30] *Evidence*, on the other hand, is translated into other languages as proof, which is a narrow fraction of the meaning it carries in English (e.g., What is the evidence supporting your claim?). The concepts beyond these terms transgress epistemology. They carry values too: it is good to formulate our ideas based on *experience* and to support the arguments with *evidence*.

Coming back to psychology, studies linking personal pronoun drop to individualism or collectivism need to be mentioned first. Kashima and Kashima (1998) were the first to report that languages that allow personal pronoun drop score higher on collectivism and related dimensions (e.g., Schwartz's *embeddedness*). Since the drop encompasses all personal pronouns, while only the *I* is of critical importance here, those results could be regarded as inconclusive. Uz (2014) was able to prove that, compared to other personal pronouns, only the relative use of *I* was related to individualism.[31] Finally, Yu and colleagues (2016) revealed an incremental trend in the use of the *I* pronoun during the past sixty years, which corresponds with cultural changes toward individuation. Interpersonal communication where partners are addressed with a singular versus a plural *you* offers another example of the same class. In egalitarian cultures such as Sweden or Spain (Schwartz, 2004), students call their professors (at any level) by their first name, which is never the case in more hierarchical regions.

In a different domain, Nisbett (2003) reported more frequent use of verbs by Chinese mothers compared to American mothers, whose conversations with

---

[30] I can attest that the expression *Canadian experience* is crucial to immigrants' adaptation in that country, particularly for getting employment. It may also appear as a tourist ad: "Experience an unforgettable Canadian vacation made just for you." No one in Poland would ask in similar circumstances for a person's *Polish experience* because it would be immediately associated with (i) the nation's war experience or (ii) the way he/she has been treated in this host country.

[31] On top of this, the English *I* is the only pronoun written with a capital letter. Contrary to this, in Polish, where the drop is practiced, capitals are used for politeness when one writes *You*.

children contained more nouns. These differences were related to the author's theory of cognitive styles: functional categorization (through verbs) in holistic East Asia versus taxonomies (noun driven) in the analytical Western world. Finally, people of different generations and religious–political orientations use different linguistic codes. Cichocka and her colleagues (2016) found politically conservative individuals prefer and use more nouns over other grammatical parts of speech. All the literature so far reported approached the language ↔ values relationship outside the context of acculturation. We will now move inside there.

Languages and values in acculturation: Problems, hypotheses, and findings. The issue of language ↔ values relationships among biculturals is a complex one. It boils down to the direction of impact: do values affect linguistic proficiency or does the level of mastering a foreign language determine personal values and identities? Various scenarios are possible:

(i)   Individuals who do not fit the normative side of their native culture may decide to emigrate, believing they will fit into the value system "over there" better, with L2 acquisition following that move.

(ii)   Learning a foreign language (L2) at home may be motivated by the high status of its culture and the gateway to enter it.

(iii)   Gaining competence in a foreign language in which the values of its culture are embedded may gradually reshape the bicultural's normative system.

(iv)   Languages are relatively separate systems that users may navigate between with no impact on the values they endorse. This is a hypothesis of linguistic-normative neutrality.

Values of another culture may precede second language learning by motivating that process. Studies from classical works by Lambert and colleagues (1984, 1993) on English-to-French immersion education in Canada, to more recent work by Chandler and colleagues (2003) are relevant here. Similar phenomena may be at work in Europe when university students choose foreign languages and cultures as majors in their academic careers. Historically, learning French in Europe meant a passage to the educated elite. In the past fifty years, English took over, not only for symbolic but also for instrumental reasons.

The culture frame switch (CFS). Most interesting theoretically is the third scenario in this list of four, where language plays an active role in spurring changes in values or facilitating their switch. Borrowing from Wierzbicka and other authors quoted in this section, certain values obtain a better representation in one language (e.g., *experience* in English) but remain deficient in the other. If that better representation occurs in L2, then these values should be enhanced with advanced language proficiency.

Since the influential paper by Hong and colleagues (2000), the CFS has been one of the central themes in the literature on biculturalism; here the leading author is Veronica Benet-Mertinez, whose works on identity integration (BII) were introduced earlier. The CFS is a fundamental mechanism operating with biculturals (Benet-Martinez et al., 2002; Benet-Martinez et al., 2006). The bond between languages or identity symbols and cognitive styles (analytical vs. holistic) was the essence of the initial studies, later extended to values (Boski, 2008). Switching from one language to another is not an unusual event, but a corresponding change in cognitive style or beliefs and values merits attention. Altogether, the three layers of culture creating my model of acculturation are inherent in Benet-Martinez's theory. The difference between the two approaches manifests itself in functions ascribed to language/symbols. For Benet-Martinez, it is limited to situational, experimental priming. In my and Kmiotek's works, language is also a relatively stable personal characteristic, measurable as L2 proficiency, and associated with values and normative identity regarded as other indices of biculturalism.

The empirical question to be addressed now is whether, within a bilingual switch, adaptive changes in values will be observed. To test these assumptions, a study was performed in Tunisia, a former French colony that remained bilingual as an independent country. In the domain of values, France is a champion of secular liberalism (see Kmiotek, 2020, Study #2) while Tunisia is a Muslim country with Koranic norms strongly entrenched in the national culture. Such conditions seemed ideal for conducting a project on the language ↔ values interface in the bicultural context of Tunisia (Boski & Iben-Youssef, 2012). We created a questionnaire of thirty-nine items derived either from the French constitution or the Declaration of Human Rights (e.g., *Enjoy yourself. Try to capture much joy and memorable moments*) or from Koranic scriptures and hadiths (e.g., *Remember that wise is the person who is a deep believer and respects the rules of religion. A fool is a faithless person*). Five questions were attached to each item: (i) this statement characterizes my family environment; (ii) if I follow this principle, it is because I am expected to act like this; (iii) if I act this way, it is because such are my convictions; (iv) this statement reflects my deep beliefs; and (v) I feel a conflict between my family environment and my convictions when following this rule. Participants who were university students or belonged to the middle-age parent category were randomly assigned to the French- or Arabic-language condition. We expected traditional values and external pressure to conform would be more readily expressed in Arabic than in French.

Results confirmed these hypotheses. Participants who filled out the questionnaire in Arabic attributed traditional Koranic values as characterizing their family environment and the self (as convictions and motivations to follow) more than those who responded in French. No such differences between language conditions occurred at the level of French individualist values. Finally, the scale of conflict between family expectations and personal wishes was more pronounced among participants who responded in French.

While the use of language in Boski and Iben-Youssef (2012) was a matter of random assignment for Tunisian bilinguals, it was a matter of personal preference in the work of Malinowska-Brokmeier (2015), who investigated two generations of Polish immigrant families in Germany: parents and their high school children. In line with our model of normative identity, parents performed the culture-descriptive part of the task (comparing Polish and German families), while their children completed scales of personal preferences, which they could do with the linguistic version of their choice. Two results of that research stood out: (i) the choice of Polish language was associated with children's stronger endorsement of Polish core humanist values and it led to better grades at school; (ii) stronger German normative identity was negatively related to the choice of Polish language, which was, in turn, responsible for adequate school conduct. In both situations, home language acquisition reflected more family care for those youngsters.

Values, symbols, and linguistic proficiency: All three combined (Kmiotek's Study #2). A study employing all three components of the acculturation model demands a rich and complex design. Its full application may lie ahead. I will report here one investigation that may encourage researchers to conduct the next attempts.

Values are most often measured explicitly by questionnaires (such as Shalom Schwartz's inventories or this author's method; also see the aforementioned studies by Kmiotek, Sharmin, and Tariq). Unlike prejudice, values always carry some positivity, but similarly to negative attitudes, values are prone to bias in self-reports. People may attempt either to hide their prejudices or to declare phony endorsement of values. This is why the Implicit Association Test (IAT), a method originally designed to measure prejudices (Greenwald et al., 1998), may be extended to the research on values. That was accomplished as part of the research program by Kmiotek (2020, Study #2) on Polish university students majoring in French language and literature.

The IAT methodology serves to establish attitudinal associations between two classes of stimuli: (i) categories represented by their exemplars (e.g., names, pictures) and (ii) trait attributes (of positive and negative valuation). The computerized procedure relies on processing their simple and combined classifications. Combined classifications can be compatible or incompatible depending on evaluation derived from category ↔ attribute associations. Take as an example people's attitudes toward two categories of animals: *dogs* and *snakes*, using a set of positive and negative trait attributes. Compatible associations occur when dogs (spaniel, shepherd, terrier, etc.) appear on the same side of the screen as positive attributes (friendly, faithful, playful, etc.), and are responded to with the same letter on the keyboard. Snakes (python, cobra, viper, etc.) and negative attributes (dangerous, venomous, deadly, etc.) make compatible classification too.

Operationally, when the position of category exemplars vis-à-vis attributes is switched on the computer screen, incompatible classifications are introduced. Participants' reaction times (RTs) to perform these tasks are measured. The *IAT effect* consists of comparing RTs for compatible and incompatible classifications. It is assumed that shorter RTs characterize compatible classifications (e.g., shepherd, spaniel ↔ friendly; python, viper ↔ dangerous) and indicate stronger attitudes, positive or negative, respectively. Incompatible associations represent rare occurrences and demand longer RTs for processing, interpreted as weaker or ambivalent attitudes.

In Kmiotek's IAT study, France and Poland were represented (i) by visual symbols (e.g., presidents: Macron|Duda; foods: *camembert* |*pierogi*), or (ii) by the first names of both genders (e.g., *Jean*|*Janek*; *Amélie*|*Magda*). We previously had consistent findings, from in-group and out-group perspectives, of Polish culture rated high in humanist (HUM) values, and French culture scoring high on liberalism (LIB) (Boski, 2006, 2012, 2022, ch. 12). Thus *caring* was an exemplary item for HUM while *tolerance* was an item indicative of LIB. In line with this logic, *Camembert* and *Tolerance* and *Pierogi* and *Caring* exemplified compatible French and Polish associations, respectively. Likewise, incompatible associations were represented by complementary compounds: *Camembert* and *Caring* for French and *Pierogi* and *Tolerance* for Polish. Finally, first names in both languages were substituted for symbols in an alternative experimental condition. The whole research session was run in either of the two languages. Figure 19a illustrates the study design.

As the results in Figure 19b demonstrate, the hypothesis whereby the IAT effect was predicted for compatible PL ↔ HUM and FR ↔ LIB associations was strongly confirmed. This is seen in the strong interaction between country symbols/first names and values ($F[1,100] = 19.55$, $p < 002$, $\eta^2 = 0.16$]. Both simple effects are also highly significant ($p \leq 0.001$). Participants responded much faster to humanist values when they were associated with Poland than with France, and to liberal values when they were associated with France than with Poland.[32]

Explicit versus implicit (bi)cultural values and identities. Since the IAT entered the research field, debate on the relations between explicit and implicit

---

[32] Kmiotek was the second researcher in our lab to obtain IAT effect on values. Earlier, Jastrzębska (2011) found Polish students responding faster to HUM values when associated with Polish first names than with Western European first names.

Psychology and Culture

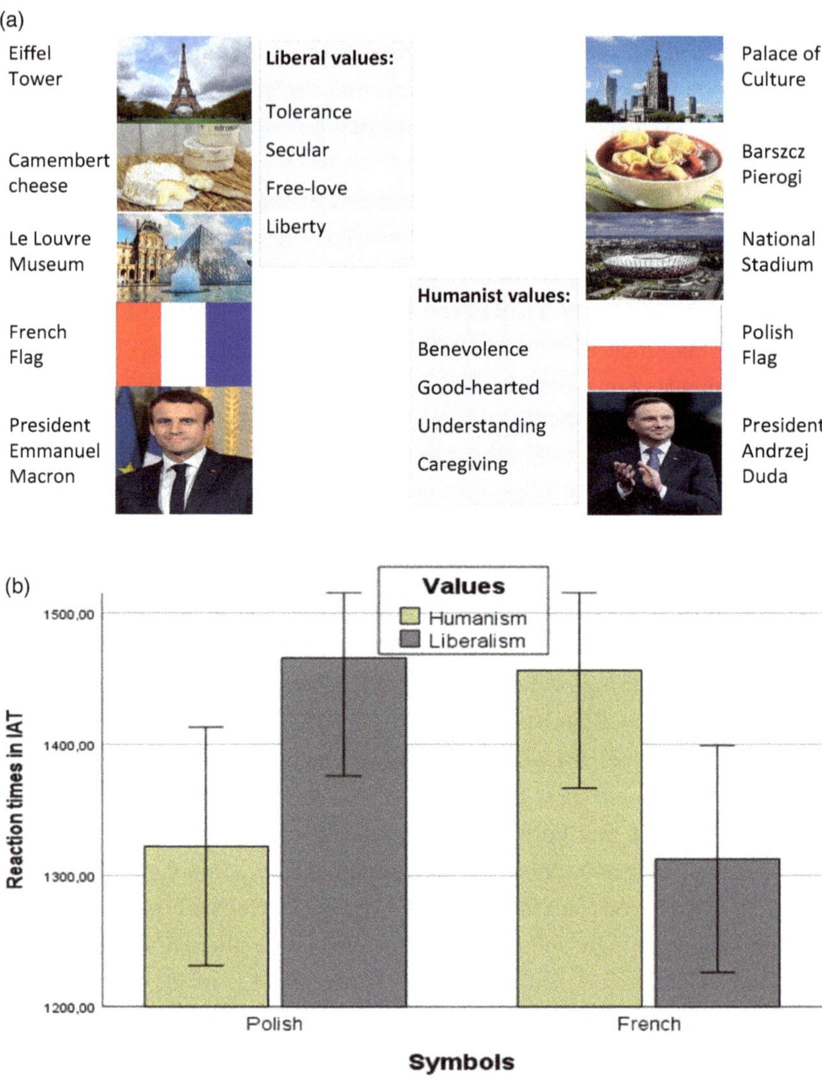

Figure 19 (a) Experimental research design and (b) IAT effect in an experiment on Polish and French symbols and values (Kmiotek, 2020).

measures has accompanied studies using both methods (Greenwald & Banadji, 2017). Explicit measures of normative identities were reported by Kmiotek (2020, Study #1), revealing the French component to be much stronger among acculturating students in Poland. Now, having the two sets of variables, the question of their cross-validation can be addressed. Generally, there were consistent, significant positive correlations between several explicit measures of culturally normative identities (joint, French, and Polish partial components) and the RTs for all value indices (incompatible and compatible) associated with France. For individuals with stronger axiologic identities, it took a longer time to connect their second culture with values. Yet, as moderation analysis revealed ($t = -2.44$, $p < 0.05$), this effect was limited to values associated with verbal stimuli (e.g., *Jean – Freedom, Amélie – Friendship*); no such effect was observed for values associated with symbols (e.g., *Eiffel Tower – Camembert)*. Figure 20a illustrates this moderation effect.

This result is contrary to a supposition linking a strong identity to short RTs. We may speculate about a possible mechanism of mindfulness operating behind these findings, arguing that participants whose cultural identities are stronger are less likely to snapshot responses associating values with unknown individuals from the C2 culture. Moreover, it is logically and psychologically reasonable to attempt a connection between a *Jean* or an *Amélie* with values such as tolerance or benevolence, while associations of this type with *Camembert* or the *Eiffel Tower* make no sense.

Next moderation revealed that the strength of the IAT effect depended on two linguistic factors: the participant's proficiency in French, and the experimental priming condition – that is, the procedure being run in French or Polish ($t = 2.70$, $p < 0.01$; see Figure 20b. The linguistic proficiency level in French spurred the relative IAT advantage – that is, the RT differences in (incompatible–compatible) value associations, provided the procedure was run in this language too. In other words, participants whose French proficiency was higher responded faster to liberal values associated with French names or symbols ($r = -0.47$, $p < 0.01$) and also to humanist values associated with Polish names or symbols ($r = -.033$, $p < 0.05$). No significant correlations were found either for incompatible sets or for Polish priming conditions. Thus culture-compatible values are more easily detected when stable (proficiency) and situational (priming) L2 conditions are met (because Polish was the participants' mother tongue, it did not make sense to use its proficiency level as a variable in those analyses). In this analysis, all three domains of acculturation are present and contribute to strengthening their consistent interrelations.

Finally, we returned to the cross-validation of our identity measures and those obtained with the BII method, presented in Sharmin (2021). French linguistic proficiency was added to previous correlational analyses between identity measures obtained in each model. It resulted in a moderation effect ($t = -2.63$, $p < 0.01$), which is illustrated in Figure 20c. Although joint Polish–French identity was responsible for the decrement in bicultural conflict (or harmony increment), French-language proficiency contributed to the steeper slope of this tendency. Selecting a foreign language and culture as a university major suggests acculturation *by desire* and perhaps a mode of cultural upgrading (similar to

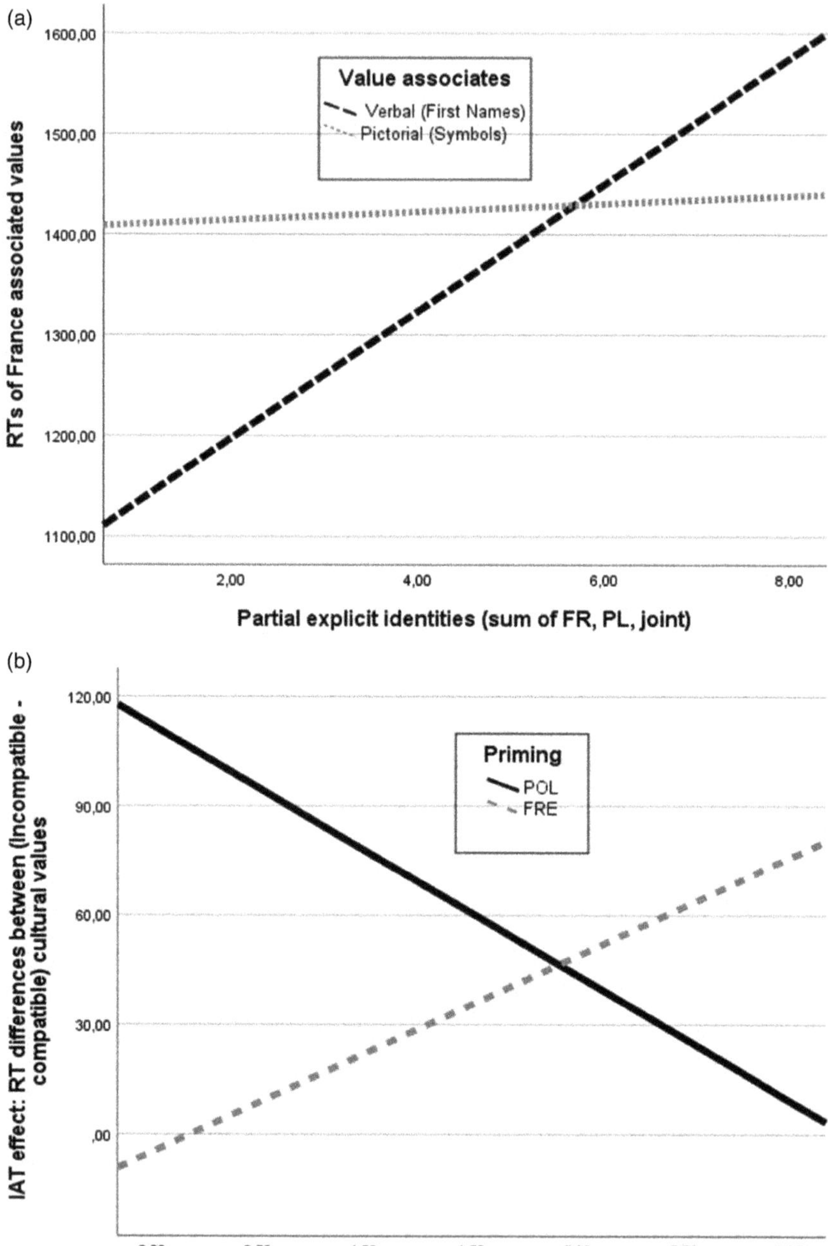

Figure 20 Moderation analyses: (a) explicit and implicit value identities; (b) linguistic L2 proficiency and IAT effect; (c) Polish–French identity and BII conflict (after Kmiotek, 2020)

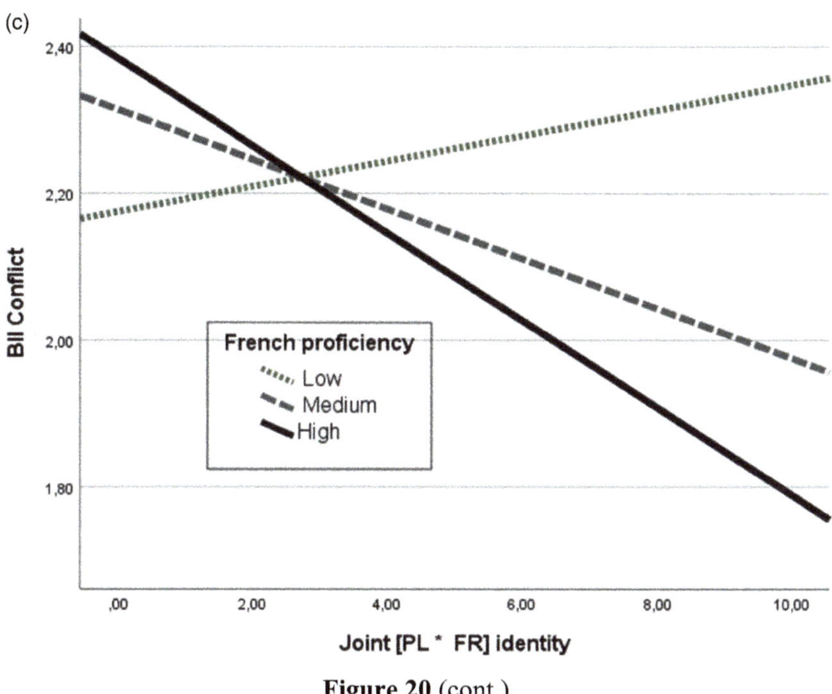

Figure 20 (cont.)

entering the EU in another study analyzed before). In acculturation *by desire*, it is not the intense L2 acquisition that induces bicultural conflict. On the contrary, it is the linguistic imbalance that disturbs bicultural harmony.

5 Discussion

Acculturation is the core section in this Element, but the conceptualization of cultural psychology came first and prepared the ground for this central theme.

5.1 Cultural Psychology and Acculturation

Cultural psychology is the general theoretical orientation that pervades this Element and all my work. Here psychological processes are derivatives of the shared web of meanings and normative imperatives that form the noosphere of human life. *To understand a person's psyche, you must know his/her culture –* is the shorthand motto of this approach. The full framework is presented in Figure 2; it not only creates a one-culture inside space but also opens individuals up to interculturality, where acculturation has been located.

The cultural experiment is the method of preference in this type of psychology. It is built around a cultural script that people have overlearned and routinely exercise in their daily lives. But what is essential here is the counter-script modification in one of its conditions. It serves to test research hypotheses through a disconfirmation procedure: expecting that participants will not bend in their actions to culturally inappropriate instructions introduced by the researcher.[33] The same counter-script function can be installed through genuine material from another culture. By so doing, in-lab cultural experiments are equivalent to acculturation experience in vivo.

Vis-à-vis any culture, people display a wide array of possibilities from full ignorance to expert competence. The way of moving on that trajectory is through the process of enculturation or acculturation. Both are culture-learning and culture-acquisition processes.

Still, a relevant question needs to be answered: why should not acculturation be regarded as part of CCP? The simplest answer is that cross-culturally we study people who (ideally) remain in no contact. But there is more to that. The full answer is provided in the flowchart of Figure 1. Typical cross-cultural research is conducted with a set of equivalent questionnaire scales intended to gauge universal phenomena. Because the stuff we use in acculturation is content-driven and measures specific competencies, the application of such tools would be counterproductive. Whatever their L1 or L2, people always speak concrete languages and they achieve testable competencies in them. It would make no sense to assess someone's linguistic competence *in general* because people do not *speak in general*. The same applies to symbols and normative scripts/practices.

This also explains why there is no need to conduct large, pancultural projects on acculturation. It would be practically impossible to gauge cultural competencies (rather than attitudes) acquired by immigrants or their children in several hosting countries. Still, middle-range investigations are advisable, such as (i) acculturation of people from several C1 home cultures in one C2 host country; or (ii) acculturation of individuals from one C1 culture in several C2s. This last remark opens up another problem, that of state-level multicultural policies, which I have addressed recently in a different work (Boski, 2023).

5.2 Changing the Contours of the Field: Subtracting Economic Migration, Adding Remote Acculturation

This proposed conceptual cleanup has intended to unconfound the heterogeneity of researched groups and problems appearing in the extant literature. For many economic migrants, their psychological adaptation to work-earn-save and remit money living conditions does not necessitate acculturation or it can occur at a minimal level. Observation of migrant communities in world megapolises

---

[33] The evidence brought from cultural experiments questions the ubiquitous power of obedience suggested by classical works like those of Stanley Milgram.

(from a Polish Chicago in Thomas & Znaniecki, 1918, until our times) proves this point beyond a shred of doubt. Our systematic research brought empirical evidence that the incremental change in hard work (conscientiousness) that occurs with economic migrants should not be subsumed under acculturation: immigrants work harder than their peers in either the home or host country for economic, not culture-related reasons. Of equal importance, this lifestyle cannot be considered an intentional *separation*; it is just a matter of different life priorities that these people define for themselves. Also, the stress they experience (work and economic uncertainty) is not of acculturative origin; it has other multiple sources: work exhaustion, legal status, worries about income stability, and meeting family-imposed expectations.

This said, it would be unrealistic to draw here an impermeable dividing line. The initial stages of minimal acculturation, illustrated in Figure 7, apply to economic migrants as a code of survival. Next, because people decide to migrate economically for lengthy periods, their initial adaptation may turn later into acculturation. The research so far has not defined any proper milestones in this process, but this is worth exploring in future investigations. I suggest that important markers here are: having children in host country schools, permanent residence/naturalization, and purchasing real estate (Boski, 2010). Altogether, longitudinal studies on the dynamics of the EARN and LEARN processes are needed to address the burning problems of economic and cultural adaptation.

Another important consequence of the existing fusion between economic migration and acculturation is the exclusion of the latter from the home country context. In his flowchart model, Berry (1997; Sam & Berry, 2006) considers foreign-language proficiency as one of the pre-acculturation factors affecting this post-migration process. I have presented ample theoretical arguments and empirical evidence to change this orientation. School foreign-language and culture learning and work in international corporate business are powerful global processes of *remote* acculturation without migration. The latter term has been independently introduced by Ferguson and her colleagues (2020), in the somewhat different context of Jamaican youth undergoing Americanization.

The sedentary, majority-group biculturals (students and corporate employees) should be of no less interest to acculturation psychologists than their peers who decided to migrate. Also, their adaptation in a broad sense should be compared with these compatriots who stick to a monocultural lifestyle. Meanwhile, I have presented evidence, coming mainly from Kmiotek's studies, that such homemade acculturation *by desire* among university students turns them into enthusiasts of the culture they study, at the expense of their native one. In conclusion, I have proposed to change the boundaries of the research territory by subtracting economic migrant adaptation and adding the in-home-country acculturation.

5.3 The Tripartite Model of Acculturation

Although it has been practiced for almost forty years, the tripartite model presented in this Element is more of a conceptual programmatic scheme than a fully formalized theory. Such a theory has not been formulated in the field. Awareness of this is an encouraging factor for its further elaboration; it opens new avenues for expansion. Four topics deserve, in my opinion, more research attention in the future.

5.3.1 Bilingualism

I will repeat the assertion that bilingualism is an inherent part of acculturation psychology, as well as the reverse statement: acculturation belongs and may enrich the field of bilingualism. The existing separation is intellectually unjustified and disadvantageous for both subdisciplines. While philological themes such as translation, proficiency, and transfer may require a special set of linguistic research competencies, it would be much harder to delineate whose is what with the issues of pragmatics and communication. Fortunately, the prolific scholarship of Anna Wierzbicka, Aneta Pavlenko, and Jean-Marc Dewaele creates a breakthrough for others. They have attempted to integrate what was before separated as linguistic and psychocultural. With bilingual individuals, it is not only the level of equivalence or imbalance between L1 and L2 that matters, but also contextual switching, barriers of mutual translatability, and domains of specialization, such as emotional experience and communication. The contrast between linguistic embodiment in L1 and its lack in L2 school learning is particularly relevant (Pavlenko, 2012). This psychological redefinition of biculturalism has far-reaching practical consequences for second-language teaching programs: away from a purely linguistic exercise, to communication pragmatics (Komorowska & Krajka, 2017). Symmetrically, it should be also reflected in intercultural competencies training.[34]

5.3.2 Symbols and Memes

There is no need to argue how powerful symbolic identity has been for individuals and groups. Strong cathexes to national, religious, and ideological symbols have led, regretfully, to dramatic events (e.g., sacrificing one's own life and killing others). Still, symbols are very important in less extreme situations too. In Benet-Martinez's culture switch theory, they appear as primers of deeper identity layers

---

[34] With its four editions, the *Handbook of Intercultural Training*, under the editorial leadership of Dan Landis, is a classic in its field. Nonetheless, bilingualism and its merger with traditional training themes is still a missing topic.

(cognition and values). But symbolic identity may be a research topic for its own sake. Over the years, our studies have unequivocally revealed that symbols carry important affective messages that support the psychological well-being of immigrants and minorities. Boski's studies on Polish immigrants in the United States and Vietnamese in Poland, Biernacka's on Brazilians in Poland, Dabee's on Mauritians, and Boski and Kurapov's on Ukrainian symbols during the current war all have been reported in the earlier sections of this Element. We propose that the mechanism responsible for these effects is the nostalgic reactivation of positive feelings, strengthening identity with the homeland (Sedikides et al., 2009; Wildschut et al., 2006).

Memes are a recent development in the cultural symbolic field, binding it with the linguistic domain. In contrast to ceremonial symbols, memes are less serious; they bring sarcasm and scorn. Yet in their dense verbal format (as puns) and pictorial transformations (as morphs), they appear as excellent sources for gauging a culture's in-depth understanding and affective attachments. With one meme, we can receive a wide range of answers, from a zero-level ignorance to a book-length story.

5.3.3 Values and Normative Cultural Identity

Our conceptual and measurement approaches to values and normative identity give a sense of novelty. Not that the term *cultural identity* is absent in culturally oriented psychology. The problem is that when used, it is ill defined and indistinguishable from social identity. For instance, in MIRIPS (Berry et al., 2018), identity items were built around country labels, in a way very similar to acculturation attitudes: *I feel that I am part of* [ethnic|national] *culture; I am proud of being* [national|ethnic]. These are affective responses to one country and the other, but I fail to see where identity is and what is cultural in these items. Colleen Ward and colleagues (Ward et al., 2018) have measured identity dimensions in a similar way, with country labels as keywords of questionnaire items (e.g., *For me, being [Chinese] and being a [New Zealander] are intermingled* = hybrid; *Who I am depends on the social context. I am [Chinese] at home and a [New Zealander]* = alternating). It would not be farfetched to claim that these are measures of broad categorical relationships but not of cultural identities.

Instead, our approach is **content driven**; it combines cultural descriptions with personal preferences, and identity is a product of these two. It offers a variety of indices (aggregate, partial) and allows multiple comparisons. The joint (partial) category often happens to be the largest in its capacity (i.e., the number of items) and it reaches the top identity valuation (Kmiotek, 2020; Malinowska-Brokmeier, 2015). This reminds us of the highest scores on integration in Berry-type studies, though the origins of our scores are quite different. Here, each value belongs to one of the four descriptive categories derived from a cross-section of two cultures, and it is later combined into an identity by multiplication with a corresponding personal preference. This enables the researcher to compute aggregate cultural identity scores (for C1 and C2) where all products are summed up. Such a procedure would be impossible with the measures of the quadruple set of attitudes [I, A, S, M], which cannot transpire into a joint score.

The most recent studies by Sharmin (Bangladeshi) and Tariq (Pakistani) have shown the mirror image distance between South Asian and northwestern European cultures; its size imposes acculturation challenges unprecedented between EU member states (e.g., France and Poland). The piecemeal approach to identity items offers a promising analytical strategy by ordering them linearly and revealing crossover points between two cultures in ascribed values and partial identities.

Our studies emphasize the importance of residence and time context in axiological identity. Idealistic identity has been reported when the target culture is not that of the current residence (Kmiotek, 2020; Malinowska-Brokmeier, 2015). Also, Sharmin (2021) found a nostalgic gap, such that her first-generation immigrants expressed a stronger home country identity than the local controls in Bangladesh. These results open a vital problem of temporal changes and their mechanisms along the process of acculturation. Are identity changes located in culture dynamics (*the world has changed around me over time*), or in individuals voyaging across cultures (*I have changed over the years*)? Are these changes objective or do they represent subjective self-deceptions or reality distortions? Our research findings suggest all of these possibilities can be at work. Future studies should delineate to what extent identity changes are externally or internally driven by the interaction of these factors.

5.3.4 Language and Values

This is the central theoretical theme, which transgresses the boundaries of culturally oriented psychology. The debate is deeply entrenched in philosophy and cognitive science. But, by studying biculturals, psychology has an important contribution to offer. Table 3 presents the problems that have been studied and those that need more work.

Most existing knowledge rests within domains: L1↔ L2 (translation, transfer) and C1 ↔ C2 (conflict–harmony, blendedness–compartmentalization), which have been reviewed in this Element. Blank spots to be addressed in future studies are located at the domains' cross-sections.

Table 3 Mutual relations between languages (L1, L2) and cognitive-normative factors (C1, C2) in bicultural individuals

Languages	Normative cultures		
	C1	**Conflict–Harmony Blended–Compartmentalized**	**C2**
L1	• [L1 C1] consistency, embodied values enculturation in the mother tongue;		L1 adequacy to process, translate, invent, and communicate C2 values
L1 transfer affecting L2 acquisition: using L2 through the L1 lens; L1 submersion in L2	• L1 specificity for expressing different religious-political worldviews		• C2 values come first and motivate L2 learning; or
L2	L2 adequacy to process, translate, invent, and communicate C1 values		• L2 proficiency makes C2 values understood and endorsed

At the L1–C1 intersection, the research question is: do people who cherish different values/worldviews speak their mother tongue differently? There is more cultural heterogeneity in values than in the official linguistic versions (e.g., dialects, jargon, slang) that people use in their mother tongue. Irrespective of dialects, there are standards of correctness in the official language. Rarely, if ever, do we still find today a (totalitarian: political or religious) society where values are observed with similar strictness. Yet, even from within one cultural perspective, we can say *the way you speak betrays what your beliefs are* (Cichocka et al., 2016).

At L1–C2 or L2–C1 intersections, we are interested to know how adequate (or lost in translation) do value expressions appear in the languages into which they need to be translated. Boski and Iben-Youssef (2012) demonstrated that the close association (Arabic–Koranic) was reflected in Tunisian participants' stronger readiness to observe those values in their original linguistic format and the context of family expectations and pressure. This proclivity was loosened up and produced conflict with autonomous motives when French was the language of data collection.

Owing to Kmiotek's research effort, we have collected preliminary findings, across domains, with aspiring Polish biculturals. Their L2 proficiency facilitated nonconflictual Polish–French normative identity. Even more important, the IAT effect of shorter RTs for culture-compatible ($FR_{primes} \rightarrow LIB_{values}$ and $PL_{primes} \rightarrow HUM_{values}$) associations were more pronounced with higher L2 proficiency. Of all reported findings, this result is theoretically the most important. It shows that improved second language performance acts as a cognitive sensitizer in detecting the proper placement of cultural values.

5.4 Conclusion: Toward a Bicultural Person

We live in a world that has become more complex than ever in all aspects of individual and societal life. From a psychological perspective, this complexity bears the name of multiculturalism (Boski, 2023). In contrast to the monocultural reality into which our ancestors were born, the (bi/multi)cultural life has already been the destiny of many people, and will be even more for generations to come. Through physical translocations and by encountering otherness without moving out, humans transcend the much smaller and homogenous environments populated by their forefathers/mothers. Being able to speak two or more languages and being meaningfully exposed to different symbolic and normative worlds create a new psyche. It is also a new challenge for psychology to update itself to this new task of understanding multicultural humans in their multicultural worlds. This Element is a small contribution to that grand scheme. It takes acculturation as a process responsible for shaping this new, bicultural psyche. In the model presented in this Element, biculturalism is considered the end product of this lengthy process (see Figure 8). It covers three domains – linguistic, symbolic, and normative/axiological – and two facets for each of them – cognitive-behavioral competencies and identity (see Figure 2). In this concluding section, I will briefly draw on potential research topics located in that framework.

5.4.1 Bilingual Competencies and Identities

Various types of bilingualism are classified and tested according to multiple criteria discussed earlier (Kurcz, 2007). It remains an open question if an ideal state of perfect, equivalent bilingualism can be reached. Mastering L2 is usually considered an instrumental task for reaching important goals (e.g., admission to an international university, obtaining a better job). The question remains, to what extent can language become a noninstrumental identity component? There is ample evidence showing that, compared to L2, L1 assumes that role in intercultural contexts. International students (and other sojourners or immigrants) search for and stick to their compatriots with whom they share their mother tongue. As the study on Ukrainians (Hrysha, 2016) revealed, foreigners may also hide their home identity in public, but this seems to be a less frequent phenomenon. More important, works by Wierzbicka (1999, 2007), Pavlenko (2004, 2008, 2012), and Dewaele (2004, 2008a, 2008b) indicate that the dominant mother tongue is more suitable for experiencing and expressing feelings verbally. To account for these phenomena, Pavlenko (2012) has proposed a developmental mechanism of embodiment. It is the *critical age* (seven–ten years) and school-learning context that restrict full-scale L2 acquisition, although it is surmountable (Tokuhana-Espinoza, 2001). In short, L1 is a more personalized language in a bilingual's repertoire, and it shapes the foundations for his/her linguistic-cultural identity. In public life, L2 is used instrumentally or as an impression management identifier; it seems to be a less likely candidate for a genuine cultural identity, including its creative use.

5.4.2 Symbolic Acculturation and Identity

Symbolic acculturation is less studied than bilingualism (Kłoskowska, 2000/1996). We may speculate, though, that the mechanism of young age embodiment operates here similarly: not only are children and adolescents taught about "our important symbols," but they also participate in family and school events where emotional celebrations around these symbols take place. It is telling that in all of our studies, positive impact on life satisfaction was limited to home country symbols. Again, with C2 symbols, there are fewer opportunities to learn about them, and affect-arousing situations are missing too. This domain of acculturation may be deficient in knowledge and the experience of embodiment.

Our world becomes symbolically globalized too. Children watch international programs with heroes and superheroes not originating from their native culture. The same happens with global sports champions and popular art celebrities. Cultural dominance manifests itself in the symbolic domain, including memes (Jasińska, 2023). It is not certain, though, if these figures or characters get cathected as cultural identity symbols in the long run. In sum, native culture seems to be providing symbolic identity dominance among bicultural individuals.

5.4.3 Normative/Axiological Acculturation and Identity

As the mainstream psychology of acculturation does not attend to language or symbols, it takes norms and values as the centerpiece of the process. As I reiterated in this Element, the value domain is least consensual compared to linguistic and symbolic. Researchers have observed that values differ more within than between cultures (Fisher & Schwartz, 2011). This statement led Shalom Schwartz (2014) to conclude that the assumption of shared values among individuals of the same culture should not guide studies anymore, and should be replaced by institutional practices. My reflection on this problem is that in most societies nowadays, there exists a variety of competing value systems, so differences are found not just between individuals, but also between the societal groups or "bubbles" (e.g., political, religious, generations) they belong to. Consequently, while entering contact with another culture requires a linguistic switch, a similar change in value orientations may not be an equivalent necessity. The system of measuring normative identity proposed in this Element merits continuation; however, the referent in its descriptive part need not be a country, but a lower-level sociocultural entity (e.g., an organization such as a corporation or a university).

Altogether, competence acquisition in all three culture layers is a condition for effective acculturation and biculturalism. As a personalized sense of attachment, bicultural identity is not a condition for a successful life but a crowning phase contributing to a sense of fulfillment. We should be reminded that the golden rule *maximum is the optimum* applies to competencies, but not necessarily to identities. There is an open space to study acculturation and the bicultural psyche in all the richness of this human experience, reaching out far beyond the current models and methods. In this final word, I should acknowledge the theoretical paradigm of Morris and colleagues (2015) which postulates fuzzy, plural cultural identities rather than bicultural identities as elaborated in this Element. Indeed, there are no compelling reasons for limiting the human psyche in the twenty-first century to bicultural functioning. The cognitive and behavioral repertoires of many people form a mosaic containing more variability than a cultural duo. Still, a transgression from a monocultural world to a bicultural world is a task of enough complexity for individual persons and researchers studying them to justify the format of this Element.

References

Adams, J. T. (2012/1931). *The epic of America*. New York: Routledge.

Benet-Martinez, V., Haritatos, J. (2005). Bicultural identity integration (BII): Components and psychological antecedents. *Journal of Personality*, 73(4), 1015–1050. https://doi.org/10.1111/j.1467-6494.2005.00337.

Benet-Martinez, V., Lee, F., Leu, J. (2006). Biculturalism and cognitive complexity: Expertise in cultural representations. *Journal of Cross-Cultural Psychology*, 37(4), 386–407.

Benet-Martinez, V., Leu, J., Lee, F., Morris, M. W. (2002). Negotiating biculturalism: Cultural frame switching in biculturals with oppositional vs. compatible cultural identities. *Journal of Cross-Cultural Psychology*, 33(5), 492–516. https://doi.org/10.1177/0022022102033005005.

Berry, J. W. (1976). *Human ecology and cognitive style: Comparative studies in cultural and psychological adaptation*. New York: Sage/Halsted.

Berry, J. W. (1979). A cultural ecology of social behavior. In L. Berkowitz (ed.), *Advances in experimental social psychology*, vol. 12 (pp. 177–206). New York: Academic Press. 10.1016/S0065-2601(08)60262-2.

Berry, J. W. (1985). Cultural psychology and ethnic psychology: A comparative analysis. International Association for Cross-Cultural Psychology presidential address. In I. Reyes-Lagunes, Y. H. Poortinga (eds.), *From a different perspective* (pp. 3–15). Lisse: Swets & Zeitlinger.

Berry, J. W. (1997). Immigration, acculturation, and adaptation. *Applied Psychology: An International Review*, 46(1), 5–34. https://doi.org/10.1080/026999497378467.

Berry, J. W. (1999). On the unity of the field of culture and psychology. In J. Adamopoulos, Y. Kashima (eds.), *Social psychology and cultural context* (pp. 7–15). Thousand Oaks, CA: Sage.

Berry, J. W. (2003). Conceptual approaches to acculturation. In K. W. Chun, P. M. Organista, G. Marin (eds.), *Acculturation: Advances in theory, measurement, and applied research* (pp. 17–37). Washington, DC: American Psychological Association. https://doi.org/10.1037/10472-000.

Berry, J. W., Poortinga, Y. H., Panday, J., et al. (eds.) (1997). *Handbook of cross-cultural psychology*, vols. 1–3 (2nd ed.). Boston, MA: Allyn and Bacon.

Berry, J. W. (ed.) (2018). *Mutual intercultural relations*. Cambridge: Cambridge University Press. https://doi.org/10.1017/9781316875032.

Berry, J. W. (2019). *Acculturation*. K. Keith (ed.), Elements in psychology and culture. Cambridge: Cambridge University Press. https://doi.org/10.1017/9781108589666.

Berry, J. W. (2022). The forgotten field: Contexts for cross-cultural psychology. *Journal of Cross-Cultural Psychology*, 53(7–8), 993–1009. https://doi.org/10.1177/00220221221112327.

Berry, J. W., Kim, U., Power, S., Young, M., Bujaki, M. (1989). Acculturation attitudes in plural societies. *International Review of Applied Psychology*, 38(2), 185–206. https://doi.org/10.1111/j.1464-0597.1989.tb01208.xbbb.

Berry, J. W., Lonner, W. J., Best, D. L. (2022). The ascent of cross-cultural psychology. *Journal of Cross-Cultural Psychology*, 53(7–8), 715–728.

Berry, J. W., Phinney, J. S., Sam, D., Vedder, P. (2006). *Immigrant youth in cultural transition: Acculturation, identity, and adaptation across national contexts*. Mahwah, NJ: Erlbaum.

Berry, J. W., Poortinga, Y. H., Breugelmans, S., Chasiotis, A., Sam, D. L. (2011). *Cross-cultural psychology: Research and applications* (3rd ed.). Cambridge: Cambridge University Press. https://doi.org/10.1177/00220221221112327.

Besemeres, M., Wierzbicka, A. (2007). *Translating lives: Living with two languages and cultures*. Queensland: University of Queensland Press.

Bialystok, E., Craik, F. I. M., Green, D. W., Gollan, T. H. (2009). Bilingual minds. *Psychological Science in the Public Interest*, 10(3), 89–129. https://doi.org/10.1177/1529100610387084.

Bialystok, E., Luk, G. (2012). Receptive vocabulary differences in monolingual and bilingual adults. *Bilingualism: Language and Cognition*, 15(2), 397–401. https://doi.org/10.1017/S136672891100040X.

Biernacka, M. (2010). Quality of life among Brazilians and Poles: Lasting differences and the situational impact of the carnival in Rio. Warsaw: SWPS University (unpublished MA thesis) (in Polish).

Bierwiaczonek, K., Kunst, J. R. (2021). Revisiting the integration hypothesis: Correlational and longitudinal meta-analyses demonstrate the limited role of acculturation for cross-cultural adaptation. *Psychological Science*, 32(9), 1476–1493. https://doi.org/10.1177/09567976211006432.

Biłas-Henne, M. (2009). Multicultural group as a buffer in adaptation processes. [Research on international students in EU member states]. Warsaw: SWPS University (unpublished doctoral dissertation) (in Polish).

Biłas-Henne, M., Boski, P. (2014). Multicultural buffer. *Social Psychological Bulletin*, (29), 179–199. https://doi.org/10.7366/1896180020142904 (in Polish).

Blumczyński, P. (2013). Turning the tide: A critique of natural semantic meta-language from a translation studies perspective. *Translation Studies*, 6(3), 261–276. https://doi.org/10.1080/14781700.2013.781484.

Bodvarsson, O. B., Van den Berg, H. (2013). *The economics of immigration.* New York: Springer.

Bond, M. H., Tadeschi, J. T. (2001). Polishing the jade: A modest proposal for improving the study of social psychology across cultures. In D. Matsumoto (ed.), *The handbook of culture and psychology* (pp. 309–324). New York: Oxford University Press.

Boski, P. (1988a). Cross-cultural studies on person perception: Effects of ingroup/outgroup membership and ethnic schemata. *Journal of Cross-Cultural Psychology*, 19(3), 287–328. https://doi.org/10.1177/00220221881 93002.

Boski, P. (1988b). Retention and acquisition of national self-identity in Polish immigrants to Canada: Criterial and correlated attributes. In J. W. Berry, R. C. Annis (eds.), *Ethnic psychology: Research and practice with immigrants, refugees, native people, ethnic groups and sojourners* (pp. 179–197). Amsterdam/Lisse: Swets & Zeitlinger.

Boski, P. (1991). Remaining a Pole or becoming a Canadian: National self-identity among Polish immigrants to Canada. *Journal of Applied Social Psychology*, 21(1), 41–77. https://doi.org/10.1111/j.1559-1816.1991 .tb00441.x.

Boski, P. (1992). In the homeland and in the chosen land: National self-identity and well-being of Poles in Poland and America. In S. Iwawaki, Y. Kashima, K. Leung (eds.), *Innovations in cross-cultural psychology* (pp. 199–213). Amsterdam/Lisse: Swets & Zeitlinger.

Boski, P. (1994). Psychological acculturation via identity dynamics: Consequences for subjective well-being. In A.-M. Bouvy, F. J. R. van de Vijver, P. Boski, P. G. Schmitz (eds.), *Journeys into cross-cultural psychology* (pp. 197–215). Amsterdam/Lisse: Swets & Zeitlilinger.

Boski, P. (2005). "Do you consent to the accession of the Republic of Poland to the European Union?" Cultural values of Euro-skeptics and Euro-enthusiasts. In U. Jakubowska, K. Skarżyńska (eds.), *Democracy in Poland: The experience of change* (pp. 243–256). Warsaw: Academica.

Boski, P. (2006). Humanism–materialism: Centuries-long Polish cultural origins and 20 years of research in cultural psychology. In U. Kim, K. S. Yang, K. K. Hwang (eds.), *Indigenous and cultural psychology: Understanding people in context* (pp. 373–402). New York: Springer.

Boski, P. (2008). Five meanings of integration in acculturation research. *International Journal of Intercultural Relations*, 32(2), 142–153. https:// doi.org/10.1016/j.ijintrel.2008.01.005.

Boski, P. (2010). Psychology migration and acculturation in a multicultural society. In H. Grzymala-Moszczyńska, A. Kwiatkowska, J. Roszak (eds.),

On- and off-road: Polish migrations to the UE after the 2004 access (pp. 107–132). Krakow: Nomos (in Polish).

Boski, P. (2012). Psychology of a culture: Humanism and social ineffectiveness embedded in Polish ways of life. *Online readings in psychology and culture* https://doi.org/10.9707/2307-0919.1029.

Boski, P. (2013). A psychology of economic migration. *Journal of Cross-Cultural Psychology*, 44(7), 1067–1093. https://doi.org/10.1177/0022022 112471895.

Boski, P. (2015). A recurring dream: African voyages. In P. Boski, J. Różycka-Tran, P. Sorokowski (eds.), *Psychological journeys across cultures of the world* (pp. 9–81). Poznan: Sorus (in Polish).

Boski, P. (2018). Explorations in dynamics of symbolic meaning with cultural experiments. In M. J. Gelfand, C.-Y. Chiu, Y.-Y. Hong (eds.), *Handbook of advances in culture and psychology*, vol. 7 (pp. 261–322). New York: Oxford University Press. https://doi.org/10.1093/oso/9780190879228.003.0006.

Boski, P. (2020). Investigating the sociocultural models with cultural experiments: A Polish–English study on {Request → Compliance} in gender relations. *Asian Journal of Social Psychology*, 23(2), 14–41. https://doi.org/ 10.1111/ajsp.12408.

Boski, P. (2022/2009). *Social behavior in cultural context: Handbook of culture and psychology* [*Kulturowe ramy zachowań społecznych*] (1st and 2nd eds.) Warsaw: PWN (in Polish).

Boski, P. (2023). Multiculturalism, social trust, and immigration attitudes [Wielokulturowość, zaufanie społeczne względem obcych oraz postawy imigracyjne]. In A. Eliasz, K. Skarżyńska (eds.), *Origins and consequences of social mistrust* [*Nieufność: Żródła I Konsekwencje*] (pp. 140–175). Warsaw: Instytut Problemów Cywilizacji Współczesnej (in Polish).

Boski, P., Antosiewicz, A. (2008). Love in novels: Preferences for authentic and fake gender characters among Poles and Americans (at home and in the other country. In G. Zheng. , K. Leung, J. G. Adair (eds.), *Perspectives and progress in contemporary cross-cultural psychology* (pp. 265–280). Beijing: Chinese Psychological Society. https://scholarworks.gvsu.edu/ iaccp_papers/9.

Boski, P., Baran, M. (2018). Poland on the map of Europe: Humanist orientation in Polish culture. In M. Drogosz (ed.), *A split social mind: Poles after 25 years of democratic transition* (pp. 25–71). Warsaw: Liberi Libri (in Polish).

Boski, P., Darpatova-Hruzewicz, D. (2023). Humanism and self-enhancement in helping Ukrainian refugees in Poland (under preparation).

Boski, P., Iben Youseff, K. (2012). Consequences of linguistic frame switching: Cognitive and emotional shifts in bilingual Tunisians. *Psychology of*

Language and Communication, 6(2), 143–163. https://doi.org/10.2478/v10057-012-0011-y.

Boski, P., Kmiotek, Ł. K., Shatruk, Y. (2020). Multilingualism and multiculturalism: Challenges for education and socialization in the XXI century. *International Journal of Socialization and Human Development*, 2, 5–25. https://doi.org/10.37096/SHDISJ-20-2.2-0001.

Boski, P., Sharmin, R., Tariq, R., et al. (2024). Acculturation: Bicultural competencies and identities. *International Journal of Intercultural Relations* (under review).

Boski, P., Struś, K., Tlaga, E. (2004). Cultural identity, existential anxiety, and traditionalism. In B. Setiadi, A. Supratiknya, W. Lonner, Y. H. Poortinga (eds.), *Ongoing themes in psychology and culture* (pp. 522–545). Amsterdam: Swets & Zeitlinger. https://scholarworks.gvsu.edu/iaccp_papers/246.

Boski, P., Van de Vijver, F. J. R., Hurme, H., Miluska, J. (1999). Perception and evaluation of Polish cultural femininity in Poland, the United States, Finland, and the Netherlands. *Cross Cultural Research*, 33(2), 131–161. https://doi.org/10.1177/106939719903300201.

Bosson, J. K. et al. (2021). Psychometric properties and correlates of precarious manhood beliefs in 62 nations. *Journal of Cross-Cultural Psychology*, 52(3), 231–258. https://doi.org/10.1177/0022022121997997.

Brislin, R. W. (1986). The wording and translation of research instruments. In W. J. Lonner, J. W. Berry (eds.), *Field methods in cross-cultural research* (pp. 137–164). Beverly Hills, CA: Sage.

Celenk, O., Van de Vijver, F. (2011). Assessment of acculturation: Issues and overview of measures. *Online Readings in Psychology and Culture*, 8(1). https://doi.org/10.9707/2307-0919.1105.

Chandler, M. J., Lalonde, C. E., Sokol, B. W., Hallett, D. (2003). Personal persistence, identity development, and suicide: A study of Native and non-Native North American adolescents. *Monographs of the Society for Research in Child Development*, 68(2), vii–130. https://doi.org/10.1111/1540-5834.00246.

Chen, S. X., Benet-Martinez, V., Bond, M. H. (2008). Bicultural identity, bilingualism, and psychological adjustment in multicultural societies: Immigration-based and globalization-based acculturation. *Journal of Personality*, 76(4), 803–837. https://doi.org/10.1111/j.1467-6494.2008.00505.x.

Cheng, C.-Y., Lee, F., Benet-Martinez, V., Huynh, Q.-L. (2014). Variations in multicultural experience: Influence of bicultural identity integration on socio-cognitive processes and outcomes. In V. Benet-Martinez, Y.-Y. Hong (eds.),

The Oxford Handbook of Multicultural Identity (pp. 276–299). New York: Oxford University Press.

Cichocka, A., Bilewicz, M., Jost, J. T., Marrouch, N., Witkowska, M. (2016). On the grammar of politics: Or why conservatives prefer nouns. *Political Psychology*, 37(6), 799–815. www.jstor.org/stable/44132928.

Chirkov, V. (2009). Critical psychology of acculturation: What do we study and how do we study it, when we investigate acculturation? *International Journal of Intercultural Relations*, 33(2), 94–105. https://doi.org/10.1016/j.ijintrel.2008.12.004.

Chirkov, V. (2020). An introduction to the theory of sociocultural models. *Asian Journal of Social Psychology*, 23(2), 143–162. https://doi.org/10.1111/ajsp.12381.

Chmielewska, I. (2015). *Transfery z tytułu pracy Polaków za granicą w świetle badań Narodowego Banku Polskiego* [*Remittances of Poles working abroad: Studies by the National Bank of Poland*]. Warsaw: Instytut Ekonomiczny (in Polish).

Chmielewska, I., Dobroczek, G., Puzynkiewicz, J. (2016). *Obywatele Ukrainy pracujący w Polsce – raport z badania* [*Ukrainians working in Poland: A study report*]. Warsaw: Departament Statystyki NBP (in Polish).

Chmielewski, J. (2009). *Language and logic in ancient China: Collected papers on the Chinese language and logic*. Warsaw: PWN.

Cole, M. (1995). Culture and cognitive development: From cross-cultural research to creating systems of cultural mediation. *Culture & Psychology*, 1(1), 25–54.

Cole, M. (1996). *Cultural psychology: A once and future discipline*. Cambridge, MA: Harvard University Press.

Cushner, H., Brislin, R. W. (1996). Intercultural interactions: A practical guide (2nd ed.). Thousand Oaks, CA: Sage.

Dabee, D. (2021). The bicultural identity and multilingual communication among Mauritians. Warsaw: SWPS University (unpublished MA thesis).

Darau, G. (2021). Local and migrant physicians in France during COVID-19: Personality, pandemic related hazards, and their mental health. Warsaw: SWPS University (unpublished MA thesis).

Dawkins, R. (1976). *The selfish gene*. Oxford: Oxford University Press.

Dewaele, J.-M. (2004). The emotional force of swearwords and taboo words in the speech of multilinguals. *Journal of Multilingual and Multicultural Development*, 25, 204–222. https://doi.org/10.1080/01434630408666529.

Dewaele, J.-M. (2008a). The emotional weight of "I love you" in multilinguals' languages. *Journal of Pragmatics*, 40(10): 1753–1780. https://doi.org/10.1016/j.pragma.2008.03.002.

Dewaele, J.-M. (2008b) 'Christ fucking shit merde!' Language preferences for swearing among maximally proficient multilinguals. *Sociolinguistic Studies*, 4(3), 595–614. https://doi.org/10.1558/sols.v4i3.595.

Dewaele, J.-M. (2010). *Emotions in multiple languages*. London: Palgrave McMillan. https://doi.org/10.1057/9780230289505.

Dewaele, J.-M., Pavlenko, A. (2001–3). *Web Questionnaire: Bilingualism and Emotions*. London: University of London. https://doi.org/10.1111/0023-8333.00185.

Dewaele, J.-M., Salomidou, L. (2017). Loving a partner in a foreign language. *Journal of Pragmatics* 108, 116–130. http://dx.doi.org/10.1016/j.pragma .2016.12.009.

Diener, E., Emmons, R. A., Larson, R. J., Griffin, S. (1985). The satisfaction with life scale. *Journal of Personality Assessment*, 49(1), 71–75. https://doi .org/10.1207/s15327752jpa4901_13.

Diener, E., Diener, M. B., Diener, C. (1995). Factors predicting the subjective well-being of nations. *Journal of Personality and Social Psychology*, 69(5), 851–864. https://doi.org/10.1037//0022-3514.69.5.851.

Doucerain, M. (2019). Moving forward in acculturation research by integrating insights from cultural psychology. *International Journal of Intercultural Relations*, 73, 11–24. https://doi.org/10.1016/j.ijintrel.2019.07.010.

Doucerain, M. (2021). Reflections on acculturation research: Taking stock and moving forward (IACCP 2021 Congress presentation – online).

Esquerra, D. (2019). *The Oshun diaries: Encounters with an African goddess*. Croydon/London: Eye Books.

Ferguson, G. M., Iturbide, M. I., Raffaelli, M. (2020). Proximal and remote acculturation: Adolescents' perspectives of biculturalism in two contexts. *Journal of Adolescent Research*, 35(4), 431–460. https://doi.org/10.1177/ 0743558419868221.

Fisher, R., Schwartz, S. H. (2011). Whence differences in value priorities? Individual, cultural, or artifactual sources. *Journal of Cross-Cultural Psychology*, 42(7), 1127–1144. https://doi.org/10.1177/0022022110381429.

Gierak-Onoszko, J. (2019). *27 śmierci Tommy'ego Obeda* [*27 deaths of Tommy Obed*]. Warsaw: Dowody na Istnienie (in Polish).

Graves, T. D. (1967). Psychological acculturation in a tri-ethnic community. *Southwestern Journal of Anthropology*, 23, 337–50. www.jstor.org/stable/ 3629450.

Greenwald, A. G., Banaji, M. R. (2017). The implicit revolution: Reconceiving the relation between conscious and unconscious. *American Psychologist*, 72(9), 861–871. https://doi.org/10.1037/amp0000238.

Greenwald, A. G., McGhee, D. E., Schwartz, J. L. K. (1998). Measuring individual differences in implicit cognition: The Implicit Association Test. *Journal of Personality and Social Psychology*, 74(6), 1464–1480. http://dx .doi.org/10.1037/0022-3514.74.6.1464.

Grigoryev, D., Berry, J. W., Nguyen, A. M., et al. (2023). Critical evaluation of the role of engaging in both the heritage culture and the larger society for cross-cultural adaptation: Multilevel meta-analyses of three multinational datasets. *International Journal of Intercultural Relations* (under review). https://doi.org/10.31234/osf.io/gf56y.

Grosjean, F. (1997). Processing mixed language: Issues, findings, and models. In A. M. B. De Groot, I. F. Kroll (eds.), *Tutorials in bilingualism: Psycholinguistic perspectives* (pp. 225–253). Mahwah, NJ: Erlbaum. https://doi.org/10.4324/9781315806051.

Grosjean, F. (2015). Bicultural bilinguals. *International Journal of Bilingualism*, 19(5), 572–586. https://doi.org/10.1177/1367006914526297.

He, J., van de Vijver, F. (2012). Bias and equivalence in cross-cultural research. *Online Readings in Psychology and Culture*, 2(2). https://doi.org/10.9707/ 2307-0919.1111.

Hecht, M. L., Andersen, P. A., Ribeau, S. A. (1989). The cultural dimensions of nonverbal communication. In M. K. Asante, W. B. Gudykunst (eds.), *Handbook of International and Intercultural Communication* (pp. 165–183). Newbury Park, CA: Sage.

Hekiert, D. (2018). Culture display rules of smiling and personal well-being: Mutually reinforcing or compensatory phenomena? Polish–North American comparisons. Warsaw: SWPS University (unpublished Ph.D. dissertation).

Hofstede, G. (2001). *Culture's consequences: Comparing values, behaviors, institutions, and organizations across nations* (2nd ed.). Thousand Oaks, CA: Sage.

Hong, Y., Morris, M. W., Chiu, C., Benet-Martinez, V. (2000). Multicultural minds: A dynamic constructivist approach to culture and cognition. *American Psychologist*, 55(7), 709–720. https://doi.org/10.1037//0003-066x.55.7.709.

House, R. J., Hanges, P. J., Javidan, M., Dorfman, P. W., Gupta, V. (eds.). (2004). *Culture, leadership, and organizations: The GLOBE study of 62 societies*. Thousand Oaks, CA: Sage.

Hrysha, Y. (2016). Assimilation as hiding self-identity: Acculturation of Ukrainian students in Poland. Warsaw: SWPS University (unpublished MA thesis) (in Polish).

Jasińska, J. (2023). Cultural identity and marital bond in mixed and monocultural couples. Warsaw: SWPS University (unpublished MA thesis) (in Polish).

Jastrzębska, A. (2011). Implicit and explicit measures of humanist and materialist values among Polish students studying in their mother tongue and English. Warsaw: SWPS University (unpublished MA thesis).

Johnson-Laird, P. N., Wason, P. C. (1985). A theoretical analysis of insight into a reasoning task. In P. N. Johnson-Laird, P. C. Wason (eds.), *Thinking: Readings in cognitive science* (pp. 143–157). Cambridge: Cambridge University Press.

Kashima, E. S., Kashima, Y. (1998). Culture and language: The case of cultural dimensions and personal pronoun use. *Journal of Cross-Cultural Psychology*, 29(3), 461–486. https://doi.org/10.1177/0022022198293005.

Kim, U. (1988). Acculturation of Korean immigrants to Canada. Unpublished PhD thesis. Kingston, ON: Queen's University.

Kłoskowska, A. (2000/1996). *National cultures at the grass-root level.* Budapest: Central European University Press.

Kmiotek, Ł. K. (2020). Polish–French bilingualism and bicultural identity: Studies on Polish immigrants in France and Belgium, and French language students in Poland. Warsaw: SWPS University (unpublished PhD thesis) (in Polish).

Komorowska, H., Krajka, J. (2017). *Monolingualism – bilingualism – multilingualism: The teacher's perspective.* Frankfurt: Peter Lang.

Kryś, K., Capaldi, C. A., Zelenski, J. M., et al. (2019b). Family well-being is valued more than personal well-being: A four-country study. *Current Psychology.* https://doi.org/10.1007/s12144-019-00249-2.

Kryś, K., Hansen, K., Xing, C., Szarota, P., Yang, M. M. (2014). Do only fools smile at strangers? Cultural differences in social perception of intelligence of smiling individuals. *Journal of Cross-Cultural Psychology*, 45(2), 314–321. https://doi.org/10.1177/0022022113513922.

Kryś, K., Zelenski, J. M., Capaldi, C. A., et al. (2019a). Putting the "we" into well-being: Using collectivism-themed measures of well-being attenuates well-being's association with individualism. *Asian Journal of Social Psychology*, 22(3), 256–267. https://doi.org/10.1111/ajsp.12364.

Kurcz, I. (2000). *Psychology of language and communication.* Warsaw: Scholar (in Polish).

Kurcz, I. (ed.) (2007). *Psychological aspects of bilingualism.* Warsaw: PWN (in Polish).

Lambert, W. E. (1984). Culture and language as factors in learning and education. In J. R. Mallea, J. C. Young (eds.), *Cultural diversity and Canadian education: Issues and innovations* (233–264). Ottawa, ON: Carleton University Press.

Lambert, W. E., Genesee, F., Holobow, N., Chartrand, L. (1993). Bilingual education for majority English-speaking children. *European Journal of Psychology of Education*, 8, 3–22. https://doi.org/10.1007/Bf03172860.

Lewandowska, E. (2008). More Polish or more British? Identity of the second-generation Poles born in Great Britain. In G. Zheng, K. Leung, J. G. Adair (eds.), *Perspectives and progress in contemporary cross-cultural psychology* (pp. 211–224). Beijing: Chinese Psychological Society. https://scholarworks.gvsu.edu/iaccp_papers/12.

Lysgaard, S. (1955). Adjustment in a foreign society: Norwegian Fulbright grantees visiting the United States. *International Social Science Bulletin*, 7, 45–51.

Malinowska-Brokmeier, D. (2015). Cultural values, identities, and psychological adaptation of Polish immigrant youth in Germany. Poznan: SWPS University (unpublished MA thesis) (in Polish).

Matsumoto, D., Juang, L. (2004). *Culture and psychology* (3rd ed.). Belmont, CA: Thomson Wadsworth.

Morris, M. W., Chiu, C.-Y., Liu, Z. (2015). Polycultural psychology. *Annual Review of Psychology*, 66, 631–659. https://doi.org/10.1146/annurev-psych-010814-015001.

Nguyen, A. M., Benet-Martinez, V. (2013). Biculturalism and adjustment: A meta-analysis. *Journal of Cross-Cultural Psychology*, 44(1), 122–159. https://doi.org/10.1177/0022022111435097.

Nisbett, R. E. (2003). *The geography of thought: How Asians and Westerners think differently . . . and why*. New York: Free Press.

Patrzałek, Z. (2020). Communicating in first vs. in second language: Cultural frame switching or compensatory mechanisms? Warsaw: SWPS University (unpublished MA thesis).

Pavlenko, A. (2004). ”Stop doing that, ia komu skazala!a!” Language choice and emotions in parent–child communication. *Journal of Multilingual and Multicultural Development*, 25, 179–203. https://doi.org/10.1080/0143463 0408666528.

Pavlenko, A. (2005). *Emotions and multilingualism*. Cambridge: Cambridge University Press.

Pavlenko, A. (2008). Emotion and emotion-laden words in the bilingual lexicon. *Bilingualism: Language and Cognition*, 11, 147–164. https://doi.org/10.1017/S1366728908003283.

Pavlenko, A. (2012). Affective processing in bilingual speakers: Disembodied cognition? *International Journal of Psychology*, 47(6), 405–428. https://doi.org/10.1080/00207594.2012.743665.

Peng, K. P., Spencer-Rodgers, J., Nian, Z. (2006). Naïve dialecticism and the Tao of Chinese thought. In U. Kim, K.-S. Yang, K. H. Hwang (eds.), *Indigenous and cultural psychology* (pp. 247–262). New York: Springer.

Pew Research Center (2017). *Remittance flows worldwide in 2017*. www.pewresearch.org/global/interactives/remittance-flows-by-country.

Piętka, K. (2015). My personality in my sibling's eyes: When the brother or sister is the home country resident or an immigrant. Warsaw: SWPS University (unpublished MA thesis) (in Polish).

Poortinga, Y. H. (2021). Concept and method in cross-cultural and cultural psychology. In K. Keith (ed.), *Elements in psychology and culture.* Cambridge: Cambridge University Press. https://doi.org/10.1017/978110 8908320.

Ramírez-Esparza, N., García-Sierra, A. (2014). The bilingual brain: Language, culture, and identity. In V. Benet-Martínez , Y. Hong (eds.), *The Oxford handbook of multicultural identity* (pp.35–56). New York: Oxford University Press.

Redfield, R., Linton, R., Herskovits, M. J. (1936). Memorandum on the study of acculturation. *American Anthropologist*, 38, 149–152. https://doi.org/10.1525/aa.1936.38.1.02a00330.

Roberson, D. (2012). Culture, categories, and color: Do we see the world through tainted lenses? In M. J. Gelfand, C. I. Chiu, Y. Y. Hong (eds.), *Advances in culture and psychology*, vol. 2 (pp. 3–52). Oxford: Oxford University Press.

Roberson, D., Davidoff, J. (2000). The categorical perception of colors and facial expressions: The effect of verbal interference. *Memory & Cognition*, 28, 977–986. https://doi.org/10.3758/BF03209345.

Roberson, D., Davidoff, J., Shapiro, L. (2002). Squaring the circle: The cultural relativity of good shape. *Journal of Cognition and Culture*, 2, 29–53. https://doi.org/10.1163/156853702753693299.

Roberson, D., Davies I., Davidoff, J. (2000). Colour categories are not universal: Replications and new evidence from a Stone Age culture. *Journal of Experimental Psychology: General*, 129, 369–398. https://doi.org/10.1037/0096-3445.129.3.369.

Rudmin, F. W. (2003). Critical history of the acculturation psychology of assimilation, separation, integration, and marginalization. *Review of General Psychology*, 7(1), 3–37. https://doi.org/10.1037/1089-2680.7.1.3.

Rudmin, F. W. (2009). Catalog of acculturation constructs: Descriptions of 126 taxonomies, 1918–2003. *Online Readings in Psychology and Culture*, 8(1). https://doi.org/10.9707/2307–0919.1074.

Ryder, A., Alden, L., Paulhus, D. (2000). Is acculturation unidimensional or bidimensional? *Journal of Personality and Social Psychology*, 79(1), 49–65. https://doi.org/10.1037//0O22-3514.79.1.49.

Sam, D., Berry, J. W. (eds.). (2006). *The Cambridge handbook of acculturation psychology.* Cambridge: Cambridge University Press.

Schank, R. C., Abelson, R. P. (1995). Knowledge and memory: The real story. In R. S. Wyer Jr. (ed.), *Knowledge and memory: The real story* (pp. 1–85). Mahwah, NJ: Erlbaum.

Schwartz, S. H. (2004). Mapping and interpreting cultural differences around the world. In H. Vinken, J. Soeters, P. Ester (eds.), *Comparing cultures: Dimensions of culture in a comparative perspective* (pp. 43–73). Leiden: Brill.

Schwartz, S. H. (2014). Rethinking the concept and measurement of societal culture in light of empirical findings. *Journal of Cross-Cultural Psychology*, 45(1), 5–13. https://doi.org/10.1177/0022022113490830.

Schwartz, S. H., Cieciuch, J., Vecchione, M., et al. (2012). Refining the theory of basic individual values. *Journal of Personality and Social Psychology*, 103(4), 663–688. https://doi.org/10.1037/a0029393.

Schweder, R. (1995/1990). Cultural psychology: What is it? In W. N. R. Goldberger, J. B. Veroff (eds.), *Culture theory* (pp. 158–199). New York: Cambridge University Press.

Sedikides, C., Wildschut, T., Routledge, C., Arndt, J., Zhou, X. (2009). Buffering acculturative stress and facilitating cultural adaptation: Nostalgia as a psychological resource. In R. S. Wyer, C.-y. Chiu, Y.-y. Hong (eds.), *Understanding culture: Theory, research, and application* (pp. 361–378). New York: Psychology Press.

Sharmin, R. (2021). Bicultural identity integration and life satisfaction: Two generations of Bangladeshi in the UK. Warsaw: SWPS University (unpublished MA thesis).

Skiba, A. (2016). Language and Stroop effect with mono- and Polish–Spanish bilinguals. Warsaw: SWPS University (unpublished MA thesis) (in Polish).

Tariq, R. (2023). Pakistani immigrants in Norway: Bicultural identities in two generations. Warsaw: SWPS University (unpublished MA thesis) (in Polish).

Thomas, A. (2002): Research into the influence of culture standards on behavior. In P. Boski, F. J. R. Van de Vijver, A. M. Chodynicka (eds.), *New directions in cross-cultural psychology* (pp. 447–462). Warsaw: PAN Publishers.

Thomas, W. I., Znaniecki, F. (1918–20). *Polish peasant in Europe and America*. Boston, MA: Richard D. Badger, the Gorham Press.

Tokuhama-Espinosa, T. (2001). *Raising multilingual children: Foreign language acquisition and children*. Westport, CT: Bergin & Garvey.

Triandis, H. C. et al (eds.). (1980–1). *Handbook of cross-cultural psychology*. Boston, MA: Allyn and Bacon.

Trompenaars, F., Hampden-Turner, C. (1997). *Riding the waves of culture* (2nd ed.). New York: McGraw-Hill.

Uz, I. (2014). Individualism and first-person pronoun use in written texts across languages. *Journal of Cross-Cultural Psychology*, 45, 1671–1678. https://doi.org/10.1177/0022022114550481.

Vignoles, V. L. et al. (2016). Beyond the "east–west" dichotomy: Global variation in cultural models of selfhood. *Journal of Experimental Psychology: General*, 145(8), 966–1000. https://doi.org/10.1037/xge0000175.

Ward, C. (2001). The A, B, and Cs of acculturation. In D. Matsumoto (ed.), *The handbook of culture and psychology* (pp. 411–447). New York: Oxford University Press.

Ward, C., Bochner, S., Furnham, A. (2001). *The psychology of culture shock.* London: Routledge.

Ward, C., Ng Tseung-Wong, C., Szabo, A., Qumseya, T., Bhowon, U. (2018). Hybrid and alternating identity styles as strategies for managing multicultural identities. *Journal of Cross-Cultural Psychology*, 45(10), 1671–1678. https://doi.org/10.1177/0022022118782641.

Ward, C., Rana-Deuba, A. (1999). Acculturation and adaptation revisited. *Journal of Cross-Cultural Psychology*, 30(4), 291–306. https://doi.org/10.1177/0022022199030004003.

Weinreich, P., Saunderson, W. (2005). *Analysing identity: Cross-cultural, societal and clinical contexts*. Hove, East Sussex: Routledge.

Wenger, S. (1990). *The sacred groves of Oshogbo*. Kontrapunt: Wissenswertes.

Wierzbicka, A. (1994). Emotion, language and cultural scripts. In S. Kitayama, H. R. Markus (eds.), *Emotion and culture* (pp. 133–196. Washington, DC: American Psychological Association.

Wierzbicka, A. (1999). *Emotions across languages and cultures: Diversity and Universals*. New York: Cambridge University Press.

Wierzbicka, A. (2007). Two languages, two cultures, and one (?) self: Between Polish and English. In M. Besemeres, A. Wierzbicka (eds.), *Translating lives: Living with two languages and cultures* (pp. 96–113). St. Lucia: University of Queensland Press.

Wierzbicka, A. (2010). *Experience, evidence, & sense: The hidden cultural legacy of English*. New York: Oxford University Press.

Więckowska, J. (2012). Personal characteristics and cultural dimensions: Consequences for psychological adaptation. Warsaw: Institute of Psychology, Polish Academy of Sciences (unpublished PhD thesis) (in Polish).

Wildschut, T., Sedikides, C., Arndt, J., Routledge, C. (2006). Nostalgia: Content, triggers, functions. *Journal of Personality and Social Psychology*, *91*(5), 975–993. https://doi.org/10.1037/0022-3514.91.5.975.

Wittgenstein, L. (2009/1953). *Philosophical investigations*. Wiley-Blackwell.

Yu, F., Peng, T., Peng, K., et al. (2016). Cultural value shifting in pronoun use. *Journal of Cross-Cultural Psychology*, 47(2), 310–316. https://doi.org/10.1177/00220221115619230.

Żywek, G. (2021). Psychological adaptation of local and international students to university organizational culture before and during the COVID-19 pandemic. Warsaw: SWPS University (unpublished MA thesis) (in Polish).

Acknowledgments

Many persons have contributed to this Element. I feel indebted for years of rewarding collaboration that led them to obtain MA or PhD degrees in psychology and allowed me to summarize our joint effort in this Element.

Dr. Łukasz Kmiotek is the author most often quoted; his work on the mutual relationship between languages and values in acculturation I consider groundbreaking, and so is his application of the Implicit Association Test (IAT) to the study of values and symbols. In the same domain, I wish to mention Agata Skiba's research extending the Stroop Test to the study of word processing among mono- and bilinguals. The experiment by Zuzanna Patrzałek revealed important differences in conversational behavior between individuals speaking their mother tongue versus their second language, which also depended on the ethnolinguistic characteristics of the observers. Deepti Dabee provided an important study on the relationship between multilingual competencies, national versus ethnic symbols, and well-being among Mauritians. Memes are popular elements of today's culture, merging short verbal and pictorial messages. Their great potential in acculturation research was demonstrated in Dr. Joanna Jasińska's research on culturally mixed marriages.

Raihana Sharmin (Bangladesh) and Rabia Tariq (Pakistan) brought the South Asian context to their studies on normative bicultural identities among immigrants from that region in northwestern Europe. They have demonstrated how large objective cultural distance is transformed into partial identities with home and host countries.

I am listing here only those students and collaborators who completed their research work in the past few years (2020+). The reader will find more names of those individuals with whom I had a chance to work earlier. Their contributions have not faded away, and I consider them all as real coauthors of this Element.

There are also three important persons at Cambridge University Press whose input in the creation of this Element from inception to completion was a sine qua non. They are Professor Kenneth Keith, the Psychology & Culture series editor; Adam Hooper, senior content manager of academic books; and Vibhu Prathima Palanisame, senior project management executive. These three editors watched over the substantive and technical quality of the publication. Thank you for your motivational support and attention to standards.

Cambridge Elements ☰

Psychology and Culture

Kenneth D. Keith

University of San Diego

Kenneth D. Keith is author or editor of more than 160 publications on cross-cultural psychology, quality of life, intellectual disability, and the teaching of psychology. He was the 2017 president of the Society for the Teaching of Psychology.

About the Series

Elements in Psychology and Culture features authoritative surveys and updates on key topics in cultural, cross-cultural, and indigenous psychology. Authors are internationally recognized scholars whose work is at the forefront of their subdisciplines within the realm of psychology and culture.